4TH EDITION
THE ULTIMATE
MARKETING
PLAN

4TH EDITION

THE ULTIMATE
MARKETING
PLAN

Target Your Audience!
Get Out Your Message!
Build Your Brand!

DAN S. KENNEDY
Bestselling author of *No B.S. Business Success*

AVON, MASSACHUSETTS

Success Reports That Tell You What You Can Achieve with *THE ULTIMATE MARKETING PLAN*

Sales Professional's Liberation

"I sell financial services to small-business owners. Your strategies took my sales business from cold prospecting and making meager commissions to over $50,000.00 a month, and now I target only ideal clients, using your direct-mail sequence strategy, and spend 80% less time working on my business! Incidentally, I'm just twenty-three years old."—**Joshua Jaouli, New York**

My kind of marketing introduced in this book is NOT just about making a lot more money. Frankly, that's too easily done. This is about how you make your money. About putting marketing systems in place of manual labor, certainty in place of insecurity, choosing clientele, and time freedom. —**Dan**

CPA Creates Wealth

"Looking back over the years (since 1996) that I began working with your materials, in a nutshell, a CPA firm that was struggling for survival is now consistently profitable and prosperous. Now, after each tax season, we have a backlog of projects for the rest of the year. We can now be selective about the people we serve. I have the confidence of knowing I can 'turn on the faucet' at will. My office is located an eight-minute walk from my home and I love hearing the morning traffic report. My wife and I live debt free; we upgraded our home, have taken vacations to Europe, Hawaii, cruises, and soon Scotland, all paid for. I've been able to counsel my second daughter and her husband on how to generate more business for their restaurant. For anyone who is a salesperson or owns a business, you make an excellent, profitable decision when you make a habit of studying Dan Kennedy's Ultimate Marketing Plan and all his other resources."—**Michael C. Gray, CPA, California**

That letter and permission to use it came unsolicited in 2005. Michael is still a Glazer-Kennedy Insider's Circle™ Member and still reporting in from time to time on the growth of his firm and personal and family accomplishments. If this book is your very first introduction to me, know that many business owners have stayed with me for five, ten, fifteen, even twenty years. Let this book be a doorway, not a dead end. Accept my invitation at the back of this book. —**Dan**

Retired NYC Police Officer—Industry Training Business

"I spent twenty years in the NYPD, for many running a real estate investing and construction business during the days while working as a cop on midnight shifts. As a result of learning your strategies, Glazer-Kennedy Insider's Circle™ membership, and Information Marketing Association membership (*www.info-marketing.org*), I started an info-marketing (publishing and training) business teaching based on my successful real estate and contracting businesses—and as this year comes to a close I'm happy to report its $930,000.00 income."—**Paul Davey, New York**

This is a great example of expansion versus growth—something made possible by mastering *The Ultimate Marketing Plan* and then applying it to one good opportunity after another. Near-seven-figure and seven-figure income is, candidly, out of reach for many single-focused small businesses, but with one business as a basis for a second, both as the basis for a third, anything's possible! —**Dan**

Retailer's Sales Struggle Ends

"My husband and I have been in retail for twenty years, and we own several different kinds of stores in our home town and two adjacent communities. We never really had the stability or new-customer-getting aspects of these businesses figured out until I discovered you, starting with your book *The Ultimate Marketing Plan*—given to me by a customer. By putting a true marketing plan in place, I have reduced our seasonal ups and downs, increased the average value of our customers per annum (measured and managed for the first time because of you), and I've become our 'creative director,' putting together quarterly promotions that bring in new customers, reactivate customers, and provide sales surges. I'm using direct mail profitably, which I could never seem to do before. And for one of the businesses, I launched an amazon.com store (at your urging) which, in its first six months, generated an extra $26,000.00. Overall, our income has doubled in a few short years. Our kids' college educations are paid with Dan Kennedy Dollars!"—**Carol Lanspa, Indiana**

My friend Mike Vance, who worked personally with Walt Disney and is the author of a number of great books on creativity, tells of asking a CEO to name his biggest business problems. When he did, Mike asked who was working on solving them and the CEO admitted no one was—because, he said, it couldn't be solved. I believe there is always something you can do. In this case, two long-standing weaknesses and frustrations in Carol's business have been solved. Too often, a businessperson gets locked in to Groundhog Day, reliving the same practices but hoping for different results. One of the best things to do with this book is to use it as a guide to see your business differently. —**Dan**

Published by Adams Business,
an imprint of Adams Media, a division of F+W Media, Inc.
57 Littlefield Street, Avon, MA 02322. U.S.A.
www.adamsmedia.com

ISBN 10: 1-4405-1184-5
ISBN 13: 978-1-4405-1184-4
eISBN 10: 1-4405-1432-1
eISBN 13: 978-1-4405-1432-6

Printed in the United States of America.

10 9 8 7 6 5 4 3 2 1

Library of Congress Cataloging-in-Publication Data
Kennedy, Dan S.
The ultimate marketing plan / Dan S. Kennedy. — 4th ed.
p. cm.
Includes bibliographical references and index.
ISBN-13: 978-1-4405-1184-4
ISBN-10: 1-4405-1184-5
ISBN-13: 978-1-4405-1432-6 (ebk)
ISBN-10: 1-4405-1432-1 (ebk)
1. Marketing—United States. 2. Sales promotion—United States. 3. Direct
marketing—United States. I. Title.
HF5415.1.K37 2011
658.8'02—dc22
2011008859

This book is available at quantity discounts for bulk purchases.
For information, please call 1-800-289-0963.

Contents

Preface

Hey, don't skip the preface!! There's important information here!
This is the twentieth anniversary edition of this book, first published in 1991. It is updated and expanded—but it has stood the test
of time, launched or greatly improved tens of thousands of businesses,
made quite a few business owners rich, and is every bit as relevant and
useful as when I first wrote it.

For the record, I'm *not* an academic theorist. I've started, built,
bought, and sold a handful of companies of my own, in vastly different
fields, and I'm always up to something entrepreneurial. As I write this,
I'm in the midst of an admittedly experimental foray into, of all things,
the mail-order ice cream business, shipping direct from the cows and
dairy in Idaho to your home or gift recipient's home or office anywhere
in the United States. I have been using everything that's in this book
personally for more than its twenty years. Further, I consult with owners of businesses small and large, and am intimately involved in their
marketing almost as if it were my own. My larger clients include companies such as the billion-dollar infomercial giant Guthy-Renker, best
known at present for its Proactiv brand (acne treatments), and Advisors
Excel, a dynamic, progressive, fast-growth financial advisor organization of thousands in the annuities field. I've helped launch a number
of companies that have found their way onto Inc. 500 Fastest-Growing
Companies and *Entrepreneur* magazine's lists of leading franchisors, in
fields ranging from tech to health care.

I tell you all this for one purpose: so you know what is in this book is thoroughly grounded in real-life experience and repetitive success, so you can confidently invest your time, energy, effort, and money in implementation of *The Ultimate Marketing Plan*.

Quickly, I'll also mention that I make my ongoing ideas, information, experiences, and advice accessible to business owners, entrepreneurs, and sales professionals via a membership program that is affordable even to the owner of the smallest enterprise, and it can be sampled free of fee—see the back of the book for more information.

So, two things before getting into the meat of this book—one, what the heck is "marketing" anyway? Two, what are the objectives in developing your own Ultimate Marketing Plan?

I'm *not* going to give you a university textbook definition of marketing —nor, by the way, is the plan presented here conforming to academic business plan or marketing plan standards, or the sort of thing you put in a fancy binder to show the banker. We're working on your business here, not trying to impress anybody or get a passing grade from some professor who has never created a customer relationship in his tenured life. So, a workmanlike definition of marketing is:

Getting the right message to the right people via the right media and methods—effectively, efficiently, and profitably.

I used to use the word "affordably"—but I've replaced it now with "profitably." The first supported most businesspeople's poor thinking about marketing investments. Most try to reach out and get customers as cheaply as possible—and, with that cheapskate thinking, rule out a lot of the best opportunities. The very first thing to understand is that the comparative *costs* of different ways of marketing are irrelevant. They mean nothing. It is the comparative return on investment translated into net profit that matters. So I now say "profitably" rather than "affordably." (For a comprehensive exploration of the numbers by which marketing should be managed and a business run, don't ask your accountant. He's a historian. Consult Chapter 43 of my book *No B.S. Ruthless Management of People and Profits*.)

This definition is, itself, worth the price of admission to this book a few thousand times over. It dissects questions about your marketing.

- **Is your marketing built around the most powerful, persuasive, intriguing, compelling, fascinating message possible?** (Or is your message ordinary, me-too-ish, dull, mundane, unexciting, plain vanilla, just-the-facts-ma'am, easily ignored, very forgettable? Or, worse, just about a commodity? Or worse still, just about cheap or lowest price?)
- **Have you determined precisely who your message should be for and figured out how to put it in front of them—quite possibly at exclusion of all others, or at least with disregard for all others?** (Or are you a vague generality, for anybody—and thus for nobody? Are you dissipating rather than concentrating your marketing firepower, trying to be noticed and heard by a population far greater in size than your resources match?)
- **Are you wisely investing in the most appropriate media for delivery of your message to the prospects in your chosen target market?** (Or are you using media because everybody else seems to be or it is popular or a salesperson arrived and pushed

you into it or because it's the way you've always operated? Note: different media are best for different businesses and different target markets at different times.)

- **Are you both effective and efficient?** (Or are you choosing the easiest or the simplest or the most efficient means out of laziness or ignorance or "too busyness" or in surrender to recalcitrant employees or poverty consciousness and cheapskate behavior?)
- **Are you accurately measuring the true, net return on investment from each marketing investment?** (Or not? Or guessing? Or carrying around opinions not verified by fact?)

If all that sounds too complex for you and your very small business, think again. When income is small, every good opportunity missed and every bad move made have big consequences. You need to be a lot better at all this than the marketing team at some big, dumb Wall Street–financed corporation. A company with 1,000 stores can—and must—do things differently than the proprietor of one, two, or a half-dozen stores. You have to micromanage your marketing. They can macromanage. They can also reach out to the best, highest-paid experts, like me, for assistance. I am routinely paid from $100,000.00 to $1 million for a marketing consulting project. That's simply beyond the reach of the small business owner, unless he is en-route to being a big business. But you must do this for yourself, and you must do it well.

If you happen to commandeer a big company, though, you should study this book most carefully and use it to challenge the marketing practices and investments being made by your minions. Big companies' marketing teams tend to be made up of people who've never had to squeeze every drop of profit from every dollar spent, who came to their jobs from the college campus rather than the street, and who are indulged rather than held ruthlessly accountable.

My objective is to equip you here with many of the basic, fundamental, most reliable marketing success factors that I use as a consultant in helping clients craft or recraft the most powerful message possible for their products, services, or businesses; choose the most appropriate media and use it in the most appropriate way; and get their message to their most valuable market. Your objective should be to put the success factors together into a plan for moving your business forward.

Personally, I detest planning, although I do a great deal of it. The entrepreneur naturally tends to prefer "Ready? FIRE! Aim." If you start muttering, "Plan? Geez, let's just go sell something," I get it. But the well-sharpened axe is a tool worth having.

—*Dan S. Kennedy*

Notes & Acknowledgments

Many of my clients, other marketing professionals, and Glazer-Kennedy Insider's Circle™ Members generously provided examples and information for this book. Throughout the book, you will see references to the Glazer-Kennedy Insider's Circle™ and its Members. This unique global association of entrepreneurs, business owners, self-employed professionals, and sales professionals share a keen interest in marketing, based on an understanding that they are all in the marketing business, regardless of their products, services, deliverables, or clientele. There are tens of thousands of Members, local Chapters meeting in many cities, major national conferences featuring extraordinary celebrity entrepreneurs like Gene Simmons (KISS), Joan Rivers, Kathy Ireland, George Foreman, etc., newsletters, online courses, and coaching programs. A FREE TRIAL MEMBERSHIP is available to readers of this book—see the offer in the back of the book.

TO CONTACT ME PERSONALLY, for business purposes or related to my speaking for your group, consulting with your company, taking on marketing copywriting projects for your business, private coaching, just to comment and share your thoughts on the book, or to report your success at implementing your own Ultimate Marketing Plan, please fax 602-269-3113 or write to me c/o Kennedy Inner Circle Inc., 15433 N. Tatum Blvd. # 104, Phoenix, Arizona 85032. (Please do NOT e-mail any of the Glazer-Kennedy or his publisher's websites. I do not use e-mail at all, and such misdirected communications rarely reach me and if they do are much delayed.)

Right Message

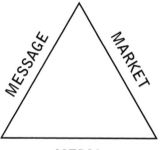

MEDIA

In 1978, when I started working as a professional speaker and seminar leader, one of the venerable deans of public speaking, Cavett Robert, sagely cautioned: "Don't be in too much of a hurry to promote, until you get good. Otherwise you just speed up the rate at which the world finds out you're no good." Harsh but good advice. It's been my observation since that large numbers of businesspeople in all fields rush to promote without stopping long enough to be sure they have something really worth promoting.

In today's incredibly cluttered, competitive environment, you need a truly great marketing message more than at any time in my thirty-five years in marketing—but it better truthfully represent what follows behind it: the prospective and actual customer's experiences.

A different expression of this same idea is this anonymous poem for advertisers:

A lion met a tiger
As they drank beside a pool
Said the tiger, "Tell me why
You're roaring like a fool."

"That's not foolish," said the lion
With a twinkle in his eyes
"They call me king of all the beasts
Because I advertise!"

A rabbit heard them talking
And ran home like a streak
He thought he'd try the lion's plan,
But his roar was just a squeak.

A fox came to investigate –
Had luncheon in the woods.
Moral: when you advertise, my friends,
Be sure you've got the goods!

Marketing—and *The Ultimate Marketing Plan*—begins not with any particular media or strategy; it starts with putting together the best, most promotable message possible that truthfully represents "the goods" you've got.

Understanding What You're Up Against, Winning the Fight with All Foes When You Must, Circumventing Competition When You Can

As you set out to construct a superpowered marketing message, you have to take a thorough survey of all you are up against—everyone else of significance who may be presenting their messages to your targeted consumer. You need to develop a message that somehow trumps all others and places you in a category of one, for the times you do butt heads. But, later in this book, we will also talk about the road less traveled—about circumventing all the clutter and competition and operating in a protected selling environment of your own making.

I'm going to suggest a little exercise to you. Stop reading here long enough to get your Yellow Pages telephone directory—if it still exists in your area—and open it up to the business category your present or planned business best fits in. You could also hop on the Internet, use search engines, and visit lots and lots of competitors' websites. Start with the first ad/first site and a thick pad of paper. Write down each promise, feature, benefit, and statement in the first advertiser's ad. When you find one of these same statements in the next advertiser's ad, just put a mark next to it, and keep stick-counting the number of times the same basic statement appears in all the ads. If you find a new or different statement in any of the ads, add it to your list, then stick-count the number of times it reoccurs in other ads.

This exercise is instructive for two reasons. First, the Yellow Pages is historically the most competitive, toughest advertising arena there is. Today, the Internet offers comparable clutter. There are ways to try and pick off searchers and direct them to looking only at your site, but as a practical matter, most who search online are sorely tempted to shop around. In both places, you are literally surrounded by competitors' advertising. With other types of media, particularly direct mail, you can get and hold one-on-one attention, deliver a complete message, with no instant opportunity and little temptation to check out what twenty or 200 others in your category have to offer. My phrase for this is "selling in a vacuum," and it is a very desirable thing to engineer.

But in the Yellow Pages, your ad is next to, above, below, and/or grouped with all your competitors' ads. On the Internet, your competitors are a millisecond's click away. You are all presenting your messages simultaneously to the same prospective customer. Here, only the strong survive; only the strongest prosper.

This is what you are up against.

Still, despite this obvious, extreme competitiveness, your stick-counted list will glaringly reveal one astounding fact: *everybody is saying the same thing.* Everybody is delivering the same message. And, with very rare exception, they are unfocused messages. They are big and broad and not really for anyone in particular.

While this seems to be the way to do things, because that's the way everybody is doing things, it is definitely the wrong approach if you seek exceptional success, even dominance, in your marketplace.

Contrary to all this me-tooism, the key to the vault in marketing in general and in these toughest media in particular is a message that differentiates you from all your competitors in a positive, appealing, preferably compelling way. Many marketing pros call this a "Unique Selling Proposition." Without this, you are merely *a* choice. With it, you can be *the* choice.

ULTIMATE MARKETING SECRET WEAPON #1: The Great USP

A *Unique Selling Proposition* (USP) is a way of explaining your position against your competition and against all other choices, actual or even imagined.

When a supermarket chain or big-box retailer like Wal-Mart labels itself as "THE Low Price Leader," they've made a positioning promise. (I do *not* recommend this lowest-price approach unless you are a giant with giant buying power. For more on price, see my book *No B.S. Price Strategy*, coauthored with Jason Marrs. Nonetheless, this is an example of a clear, forthright, definitive USP.)

A USP is also a way of summarizing and telegraphing one of the chief benefits of the business, product, or service being marketed. When I wrote the first edition of this book in the early 1990s, Chrysler was making much out of being the only American carmaker to include driver's-side airbags as standard equipment. That briefly worked for them as a USP, but competition quickly caught up. More recently, and I think humorously, the Subway chain enjoyed great success repositioning itself as a weight-loss business with Jared's story. How long they can sustain this is open to question. Taco Bell briefly tried copying this idea, but it seems people are unwilling to see burritos and tacos as a weight-loss diet. Anyway, historically, and contemporarily, most great businesses put forward Unique Selling Propositions—or at least try to.

Your USP may express the theme of your business, product, or service.

Think: Which coffee is "mountain grown"? Which beer is made with "the clear, cold water of the Rockies"? Where is "THE Happiest Place on Earth"?

We dubbed Glazer-Kennedy Insider's Circle™ THE Place for Prosperity™, in keeping with the fact that entrepreneurs often feel odd-man-out, isolated, misunderstood and underappreciated, and are encouraged by having a place of their own, where leaders and peers truly understand them and support their endeavors. That's half the theme of our membership. The other half is unapologetically about making money, making more money, developing wealth. Actually, all the above USPs reference "place".

These examples show that a USP can be based on just about anything: price, product positioning, place. There are USPs based on color, size, scent, celebrity endorsement, location, hours of operation, and on and on. The most obvious is, I suppose, being number one. When you are number one, though, as with all marketing messages, care must be given to match the message with the audience. As an example, here is a number-one-position/trust USP that I developed for my client

Guthy-Renker for its Proactiv acne-treatment products. But recognize that it is for the parent customer, not the actual teen user. To teens, at their age, credibility is a nonstarter. It has little or no persuasive value. But for moms, it is enormously persuasive.

> Doctor Developed. Teen Proven. Mom Approved. Acne Treatment that works. The only acne treatment that prevents new break-outs. Guaranteed.

As you concentrate on developing a new USP for your enterprise, you'll be newly aware of the USPs of other businesses, and you can learn from their examples. To hone your marketing mind, you need to become USP-sensitive and ask these questions about every business, product, and service you encounter in your daily activities:

1. Does this business have a USP?
2. If not, can I think of one for it?
3. If so, is there a way I can think of to improve it?
4. Is there any idea here I can borrow for my use?

How a Terrific USP Built an Entrepreneurial Empire

I've used this example for more than fifteen years—it's that good. Once upon a time, two young men determined they would put themselves through college by running a small business. Early on, the business was woefully unsuccessful, and one guy bailed out on the other. Tom Monaghan, the one who stayed and stuck it out, came up with a USP that revolutionized his entire industry and made him a multimillionaire. First, his little business grabbed dominant control of the local market. Then, rapidly, his state, America, and then the world! The right USP core of the right marketing message can give you dominance in a small pond or even take you from local to global, small to gigantic.

The USP was: "Fresh, hot pizza delivered in 30 minutes or less, guaranteed." Ten words that brilliantly incorporate two product benefits, the **meaningful specific** of delivery within 30 minutes—not "quick," "fast," "soon," but *precisely* in thirty minutes, and a **guarantee**. This USP has passed into advertising history, but it fueled the growth of an empire and thoroughly frustrated competitors large and small. In fact, in its heyday, I played word association with people and asked them to say whatever first popped into their minds when I said "pizza," and 85 out of 100 said: "Domino's."

Question: If we went out into your marketplace and asked 100 or 1,000 people to play the game, gave them the generic name for your type of business, and 85 percent of them responded by naming you, how well would you be doing?

I had the privilege of interviewing Tom for a magazine article, and there's no doubt that his success and that of his company has been linked to a complex list of factors, notably including his personal success philosophy and his ability to instill it in his franchisees. Today, the company has grown far beyond dependence on Tom's influence and is about system, geographic coverage, size, as well as consumer familiarity with the brand. But there's also no doubt that his USP was largely responsible for the rapid rise and dominance of his company in the pizza industry. It generated enough wealth to let Tom indulge his lifelong fantasy of buying the Detroit Tigers (with a $53 million price tag), collect classic cars, give most generously to his church and favorite charities, and be financially independent and secure at a relatively young age.

That is the power of a truly great USP. It *is* worth working on the invention of a strong USP for your product, service, or business. And it's not necessarily easy. I know clients who've taken months, even years, to finally hit on a USP that they liked and that really worked. For each, the months of frustrating brain strain have paid off handsomely.

I should point out that you can go to very different places in the same industry with a USP. In the pizza business, one of our most celebrated

Members is Diana Coutu of Diana's Gourmet Pizzeria, a thriving business dominant in its market, but at premium price levels—upwards from $25.00 for a large pizza—and all about gourmet quality, not speed, not price. You'll hear more about Diana later in the book.

Products That Have USP Power

The Christmas shopping season always brings forth a crop of interesting new kitchen appliances—one year it was the Iced Tea Pot. When I first saw this advertised, I burst out laughing. Its manufacturer went laughing all the way to the bank. Imagine: we can no longer make iced tea in any old kettle; we must have the precisely correct Iced Tea Pot.

It reminds me of a funny phenomenon in the Southwest: the Sun Tea Jar. Because there's searing sunshine every day, it's easy to sun-brew tea just by putting a large jar of water outside for a few hours with tea bags in it. Obviously, any old glass jar will do the job. But on store shelves you'll find large glass jars with the words "Sun Tea Jar" silkscreened on them for sale at four or five times what unmarked jars in the next aisle sell for. And you'll find people cheerfully buying them. After all, what kind of goofball would brew sun tea in a pickle jar?

Purely through customized or proprietary appearance, these products have taken on a USP POWER that is almost invincible.

If you really want to see this at work, visit an athletic-shoe store. I'm not much of a casual dresser, but, immediately before a day of walking at Disney World, I decided it would be smart to get some comfortable sneaks. Forty minutes and eighty-five bucks later, I left the store with a thorough education: there are shoes for walking on pavement, for walking on grass, for walking a lot, for walking a little, for jogging, for tennis, basketball, soccer, football, baseball, trampolining, with pumps, without pumps—but there are no more sneaks.

Consider these products with USP POWER:

- Microwave dinners: for kids to make for themselves
- A stress management seminar: for career women
- A shampoo and conditioner: for swimmer's hair

In these instances, the USP is based on who the product is for, and by a specialization that is more illusion than reality. Stress management techniques are stress management techniques. My wager, based on extensive experience with clients in the cosmetic, beauty, and health product fields, is that the ingredients in the shampoo for swimmer's hair are nearly identical, maybe identical to those in other shampoos. There is a nutritional supplement formulated to improve eyesight sold under one name and label to hunters, a different name and label to sewing and quilting hobbyists, and yet another different name and label to pilots. The pill is the same in all three bottles. The difference is entirely in the marketing.

There are, of course, actual specialization-based USP products. Diana, mentioned earlier, has pizzas specifically for diabetics that are made with different ingredients than the other pizzas.

The important thing to understand about this USP pathway is that people very much want to believe that they are unique and that there is something specifically formulated, engineered, designed, or customized just for them. The "Hey, that's for ME!" reaction to a marketing message moves the person toward purchase quickly and decisively, and has the added virtue of making price elastic. This is, then, a very good USP question to ask yourself about your marketing message: Does it make someone perk up and say "Wow, that's for ME!" ?

The Productization of a Service Business, Another Path to a USP

Service businesses deal with intangibles; product providers deal in tangibles. Because it is generally easier and simpler to convey value in marketing tangibles than intangibles, one of the cleverest paths to a USP is to productize services. A great example comes from a tremendously successful Glazer-Kennedy Insider's Circle™ Member, Grant Miller, owner of Sun Your Buns, a chain of tanning salons in Pennsylvania. I've reprinted an entire article about his business from the Glazer-Kennedy Insider's Circle™ NO B.S. MARKETING TO THE AFFLUENT LETTER (one of several different marketing newsletters published by Glazer-Kennedy Insider's Circle™. For more information, refer to the back of this book) in the Bonus Chapters at the back of this book, because he demonstrates what having a *complete* Ultimate Marketing Plan is all about. On the following pages, however, I'll just briefly describe his productization strategy and show you one example—his membership offerings.

As the illustration that follows shows, there are six different Sun Your Buns memberships, each with a different collection or combination of services and use privileges, each at a different monthly price, automatically charged to the member's credit card each month. That's a side point not to be overlooked: automatic, reoccurring income, with payment made on the first day of each month *before* any services are provided. Anyway, this shows how intangible services can be organized and packaged into tangible product, in this case, membership.

*The NO BS MARKETING TO THE AFFLUENT LETTER is one of several different marketing newsletters published by Glazer-Kennedy Insider's Circle™. For more information, refer to the back of the book.

To the Prospective Customer's Question, Your USP Is the Answer

When you set out to attract a new prospective customer to your business for the first time, there is one paramount question you must answer— my proprietary, copyright-protected USP question.

Ask yourself: **"Why should I choose your business/product/service versus any/every other competitive option available to me?"**

I invented this question to help businesspeople understand what a USP is and to use as a crowbar to pry ideas out of their heads, to dig out the makings of a good USP. If you can't answer the question, you won't get a USP, but you also have bigger problems—typically it'll mean that you've been getting your customers only because of cheapest price, convenient location, your personal smile-n-shoeshine charisma, or the good fortune of being the only provider, and all these leave you very, very vulnerable to new competition. You *need* a USP.

Grant Miller Membership Offerings Example

One side of the two-sided sales card shows the membership levels (from $18.88 to $98.88 per month) and pictures of the different tanning booths included with each level. The reverse side (not shown) displays the benefits first-time members receive upon joining—at Premiere level, a free weekend cruise. To save you the math, this puts a twelve-month sale at $226.56 to $1,186.56, plus product purchases, one-time upgrade purchases, and ancillary revenues, such as tooth whitening or laser skin treatments.

Boosting USP Power with an Irresistible Offer

I grew up in Ohio and briefly owned an ad agency in a rural community halfway between Cleveland and Akron. At least a dozen times each winter there was enough snow and ice on the country roads to make it ill-advised if not downright impossible to go anywhere. Those days the office stayed closed and I stayed stuck at home. It was a much bigger deal then than now: Then, no one had a computer at home, and there was no Internet, no real ways of working effectively if locked out of the office.

On one such day, in the midst of a severe blizzard, I stared out my apartment window and watched a neighbor slog through the snow, struggle through the wind, scrape ice from his car's windshield, unfreeze the car's door latch with a cigarette lighter, fight to start the car, and finally slip and slide off into the storm. "I wonder," I asked myself, "what would motivate a guy to go out in weather like this?" Marketing is really about motivating people to action, often into doing something they would not do purely of their own initiative.

Then I remembered a very similar storm just a couple of winters before when I had quite literally risked my life and badly banged up my car driving all the way from Akron, Ohio, to Murray State University in Kentucky to spend a weekend with my girlfriend of that time. For hours, it snowed so hard I honestly couldn't see past the hood ornament of my car. Every bridge was so icy I spun my way across it. Yet I pressed on.

Why? Waiting for me in Murray, Kentucky, was "an irresistible offer!"

It was, as I recall, stated in twenty words that cannot be published here.

If you can come up with an offer *that* irresistible, you are really on to something! Try this one on for size: for $198.00 per person, $396.00 per couple, I'll put you up in a luxurious minisuite in an exciting Las Vegas hotel, right on the famous Strip . . . give you tickets to a show with famous entertainers . . . put a chilled bottle of champagne in your room . . . let you drink as much of whatever you want whether you're at the gaming tables, playing the slots, or in one of the lounges . . . hand you

$1,000.00 of my money to gamble with ... let you keep all your winnings ... and, as a bonus, guarantee you'll at least win either a TV or a faux-diamond ring. Obviously I'm not going to give this incredible deal to everybody in the whole world. There can only be a small number of these vacation packages available, first come, first served, and the race is on. Assuming you trust the offer, how fast can you get to a phone and call in to reserve yours? Would you go out in a blizzard and drive to the post office to get your order form in the mail before the deadline?

Well, this was a real offer, from Bob Stupak, the entrepreneurial owner of the original Vegas World hotel (now the Stratosphere) and one of the savviest marketers I know ever to take on Las Vegas. For years, Bob kept his hotel filled to capacity, kept a waiting list going, and got paid months, even years, in advance by his guests—all thanks to his invention of this irresistible offer. He used the cash flow generated by selling that package to grow his hotel from a tiny, slots-only joint to a huge, two-towered showplace. After Bob sold out, his kind of marketing exited with him, so you won't see it on display today.

Sometimes the most irresistible offer is free, sometimes not. You can see our own very successful free offer at Glazer-Kennedy Insider's Circle™ by accepting the invitation at the end of this book.

Either way, with free or with an over-the-top, stacked-benefit offer like Stupak's, you are using a value-driven USP.

Being in the Right Place at the Right Time with the Right USP

Once, over a lengthy lunch, I listened to a client, Ned Allen, then a developer of planned retirement communities, reminisce about his role in starting the famous Steak and Ale restaurants smack in the middle of a national recession. He had started the first restaurant with just $2,000.00, made it successful, and committed to the construction and opening of seven new restaurants just as the recession hit.

Ned said: "We had to quickly change our thinking to match the timing we had to work with. We developed new, lower-cost, higher-perceived-value menu items, and by offering the look, feel, atmosphere, and taste of a gourmet steakhouse at a surprisingly low price, we had the right product at just the right time."

As I was writing the first edition of this book, Ned was not alone in predicting another three- to four-year-long recession, and he was again busy creating just the right product for it. In this case it was a new type of a manufactured home for his companies' communities—this one with several hundred square feet less than any other home and, therefore, a substantially lower cost but an interior design that made it seem much, much bigger than it was and that had lots of nifty "gingerbread" touches that added to its perceived value.

Ned turned his $2,000.00 investment in Steak and Ale into over $5 million when he sold out to Green Giant Foods. He then made another fortune with his new "Land Yacht" mini retirement home and his inventive approach to low-cost retirement living in Florida.

Of course, it's no secret that timing is a business success factor. But matching a USP with the right timing can dramatically multiply success. **There are two basic approaches to timing and to a timing-oriented marketing message.**

One is, as Ned did with Steak and Ale, adapt the business to the opportunity or mandate of the moment. He altered his plan for an ultra-upscale steakhouse to put forward a product ideally suited to the circumstances of the moment. In taking such an approach, you have to believe the circumstances of the moment are an opportunity, with at least several years' life to them, and a way to come out of the backside of those circumstances with a business flexible enough for long-term success.

The other is to get into a business based on timing factors. Recently, I entered into a complicated, three-way consulting relationship with a marketing expert in the financial services industry, Matt Zagula, and a fast-growth annuity field sales organization of about 1,000 agents but primed to double in size, Advisors Excel, specifically because of timing and trends. Their target market is trailing-edge boomers and seniors of a conservative investment mind, motivated by safety, security, preservation of savings (bluntly: not running out of money before they die), and trustworthy advice. The combination of the peaking of that population of prospective clients; the huge amounts of idle, investable assets they control; and the fear and anxiety engendered in them in the 2009, 2010, and into 2011 ongoing recession and economic turmoil here and abroad, Washington's discussions of rejiggering Social Security, Obamacare, and on and on is, from a marketing standpoint, a truly perfect storm. Thus, from my standpoint, it was the ideal timing to invest a lot of time and effort in this industry.

How "Marketing by Values" Strengthens Your Message

One of my first mentors in business often said: "If you stand for nothing, you'll fall for anything." Just about anything—recession, new competition— can topple a business devoid of values.

Although there are many great success stories in the fast-food industry, none stand above McDonald's. The McDonald's empire was built on Ray Kroc's unwavering, some would say fanatical, commitment to *consistency*—the idea that the food items at a McDonald's in Iowa are identical to those found under the arches in California. Try to find anything close to this kind of consistency in any other national restaurant chain. A few have finally gotten close. But it took them decades to get there.

Federal Express invented, built, and dominated an industry because of a commitment to on-time, as-promised delivery, and there are many classic stories of FedEx employees going to extraordinary extremes to keep faith with this fundamental value. Of late it seems to me, as someone who spends tens of thousands of dollars a year with FedEx, that their reliability is slipping, and I hope they are not letting go of their core value in surrender to logistical or cost or poor workforce quality influences.

Peterman Catalog Page Example

In my *No B.S. Marketing to the Affluent* book, I featured J. Peterman. If you are not familiar with the famous J. Peterman catalog, please visit *www.jpeterman.com*. He and his team are scary good at making a product about something much more than it is by tapping into peoples' emotions, emotional connections, and values.

For example, one of his catalogs recently included a $159.00, essentially ordinary varsity jacket. (Catalog page shown here.)

You can buy well-made, nice-looking ones in many different places for a third of this price—but, then again, it might never have occurred to you to want or buy such a jacket like this unless Peterman's catalog arrived in your mailbox and got you interested. I certainly had no such pre-existing interest, yet this nearly got me, and the only thing stopping me was the fact that I already own a varsity-style jacket as well as more autumn-weight jackets than

I need or can wear. But I had a friend and business associate who was an Andover grad, who took me there for a visit, and this copy made me think of that storied, other-world campus, then of my visit to Notre Dame, then of High Point University, where I am on the advisory board of the School of Communications. As somebody who never attended a prep school or a college, I have a nostalgia for it that is imagined rather than experienced. I miss football games never attended.

Being young again is what's being sold here—*not a jacket.*

This is about how somebody in his forties or fifties or so is going to *feel* when wearing this jacket. It's a time machine, not apparel. Peterman's words: "young . . . invincible." That's how getting into my '72 AMC Javelin AMX makes me feel. It takes me back to a time when I roared along back roads without thought of speeding tickets or points on my insurance or avoiding accidents; I was invincible then. At certain ages, I imagine just about everybody is eager for this feeling, then different people go about trying to buy, rent, or get it via different ways—but are probably susceptible to being sold it in many different packages. A whole lot of people have no *need* for an autumn-weight jacket (or a classic automobile, such as I own), and many people, as an act of responsibility, resist buying things they do not need, especially in a recession or postrecession hangover. But feeling young again transcends need. It is even more powerful than a mere simple want. It is a *transcendental* promise.

It's important to understand that most people won't actually *do* much of anything to make such an ideal a reality.

Most will not, for example, convert to a severely calorie-restricted Mediterranean diet, exercise for thirty minutes every day, stick to a complex regimen of nutritional supplements, relocate to a less stressful and less toxic place, and so on in order to feel young again. But if they can buy something and scratch the itch (or awakened-for-them itch) by a simple, nontaxing act—be that a yo-yo on impulse at the grocery checkout or this jacket, or for the more affluent, the sixty-year-old fellow who acquires the twenty-two-year-old wife (or, I suppose, vice versa)—lots of people will make a purchase to feel young again. Youthfulness—the appearance of it, the feeling of it—is a highly prized American value.

I was recently visiting with one of my literary agents who, some five years ago, longing for the simple life, moved from New York City to a town of 1,100 people in the Berkshires where every day he walks short distances from his home to office to diner to post office (because there is no mail delivery). He sits in his yard and sees wildlife and looks up at the stars. He does not hear the police sirens and street noise of the city. There are no giant piles of garbage bags every few feet on the sidewalks. He sees his neighbors picking up their mail, at the dump (where everyone drops off their own garbage), at the hardware store. He has a quiet and calm and simple life, very simple.

This life appeals to me a great deal. But I am not going to abandon my entire life, notably including what is place linked, on a whim and disappear to a similar town, at least not now. But I might buy a big picture book or DVDs or some product symbolic of such a place or life, or maybe a flannel jacket and walking stick sold by Peterman and favored by the folk in such a place. I won't do anything about this impulse. But I might buy something because of the impulse.

Many people associate small-town life, nostalgically remembered or imagined, with treasured values: simplicity, honesty, family. Such people often buy things that connect them to that life. A long-time client of mine, Darin Garman, who markets investments in apartment buildings and commercial properties in Iowa to people all over the world, most investing from a distance in properties sight unseen, relies heavily on the concept of "heartland of America" real estate and on the description of his life and times in the quintessential American small city, Cedar Rapids, Iowa, in his marketing messages. Many of his investors have heartland of America roots and family connections but now live in New York or Los Angeles or Washington, D.C., or overseas.

How to Connect with Moms

Here are the **facts**. Heritage brands that have been around a long time score big with moms—they have a preference for brands they grew up with. Leadership position comes in as close second: being number one equates to quality, value, and trustworthiness (thus you want to construct a category you can be number one in). In addition, 87 percent of moms reported being interested in advertising images of moms having fun with their kids; 86 percent appreciate seeing their multitasking acknowledged. (Sources: The Parenting Group – Survey; AskSmartyPants.com; BIGresearch.com; Marketing to Moms Coalition.org). Moms have a values image that—even though they may not conform to it in actual daily life—is at least an aspiration, if not a fiction, they imagine themselves and their family in. A marketing message promising this fiction as an outcome can be very persuasive.

I am working now with my client, Alan Reed, to build a similar "Andy Griffith-y" simpler-life storyline into the marketing of his dairy farm's ice-cream-of-the-month clubs to consumers all over America, under the brand of Reed & Kennedy Farm Fresh Ice Cream, which you can see at *www.ReedsIceCream.com*.

It's important to understand that just about any product or service can be linked to values. Following is some copy I've written for use in advertising Proactiv acne treatment products to moms. Obviously, the copy is not about the product but about their role as mothers.

"MOM" COPY SAMPLES

Again, she says, "I'd rather stay home." Mom, does your daughter hide her face—*and cry?*

Will these years be your teen's *best* years? So many firsts: first job, first date, first kiss, first relationship. The real world will take over soon enough. There's no reason to let your daughter's acne ruin any of this. When they look back on these years, every Mom hopes her daughter will have wonderful memories. But acne, it's constant and the embarrassment it causes can, pardon the word, blemish these years—unnecessarily, because there is a Doctor-developed, teen-proven, Mom-approved and guaranteed in-home treatment . . .

What's Your Magnificent Mission?

The nature and details of my business interests have changed quite a bit over time, but I've always kept them linked to this mission: to be responsible for getting how-to-succeed education into the hands of more people than any other individual or enterprise.

At one time I saw the implementation of that mission limited to the mail-order marketing of books and courses. Then it expanded to include speaking and seminars. Then television. Then developing products for other publishers. Then consulting with publishers and direct marketers, even the birthing and expansion of an entire industry now known as information marketing, represented by the Information Marketing Association (*www.info-marketing.org*). And, now, through a network of consultants and marketing advisors to hundreds of different industries, businesses, and professions, I get success education and marketing systems into the hands of more than 1 million business owners every year.

All of this gives most of my business activity some meaning greater than just getting money into the bank accounts. From that comes, I think, a different, superior level of creativity, inspiration, and persistence. There is also a general sense among all my clients and customers and subscribers and readers that we are, together, about something more than me as merchant, they as consumers, and money changing hands. Without it being inauthentic, I think this is an important aspect of a sustainable successful business or career, and something that greatly strengthens marketing messages.

Oprah is, I believe, the wealthiest entertainer of our time, certainly the wealthiest television personality. But her long-running daytime talk show, the foundation of her business empire and fortune, definitely seemed to be about something more than just a show or a paycheck, however large. She has been a champion of a philosophical position, and of numerous causes. Trump's main real-estate business has been about "forever changing the skyline of New York," and the recent years' brand-development exercise has been about "representing the best." I recently stopped into a little shop on Main Street in Hudson, Ohio, for a cup of coffee to discover that the Hattie's shops—that one and several others—all employ developmentally challenged young people and support related activities like the Special Olympics.

I'm not necessarily saying that you have to have some saintly charitable or profoundly philosophical motive behind your business activities. And I'm not one who feels any guilt about making large amounts of money. But I do find that the business owner who is at least as enthusiastic about the values and mission and processes of his business as he is about its bank balance does best.

Walt Disney was thrilled when he finally achieved significant financial success, but he was much more committed to his ideals for his theme park than he was to piling up personal wealth. Once, driving home, he noticed an attractive new car in a showroom window and thought to himself: "Gee, I wish I could afford that car." He drove a few more blocks before realizing, "Hey, I *can* afford that car!"

I think you'll find the challenges of successfully crafting and conveying great marketing messages easier and more fun to meet when you are on a magnificent mission!

It's Time to "Assemble" Your Message

To clarify, your marketing message is the story you are going to tell about your business in your advertising, marketing, online and offline media, in direct mail, conversationally, by every means. At its core will be a foundational, permanent message that you convey consistently. At different times, for different purposes, you may hook different offers, propositions, promotions, or enhancements to it. For different audiences, you may customize it. Always, though, you will be telling a story centered around the most complete and compelling USP you can create.

You have undoubtedly had the "joy" of opening a large box and laying out a hundred parts, pieces, screws, and bolts on the floor and trying to assemble them into the beautiful bookcase or computer workstation or whatever is pictured on the outside of the carton. Well, there you are again, only with pieces of a marketing message. Actually, that's where you start. Keeping in mind everything we've discussed in this chapter, get a large pile of blank 3" × 5" cards and start putting one fact, feature, benefit, promise, offer component, and idea on each card—until you have, over a series of brainstorming sessions, exhausted everything you know about your business and its competitors. Then do your best to prioritize the items, in order of their probable importance to your customers and their contribution to differentiating you from your competition. Through this exercise, you can come to the creation of the best possible USP, a supporting sales story, and one or more related offers.

Presentation

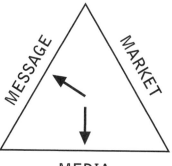

MEDIA

Regardless of the target markets you later select—or, preferably, may have selected before you developed your message—and the modifications you make in your message to fit these markets, and regardless of the media mix you use to deliver the presentation of your message, there are some key ideas to keep in mind about making the right presentation.

The Battle to Communicate

There is a now very old, true, and still instructive story about Stew Leonard's famous super-supermarket, where they were bringing in fresh fish every day, carefully packaging it, and displaying it in their freezer cases, clearly and proudly labeled as FRESH FISH.

They had the right message—people who like fish really like *fresh* fish. At the time, few other supermarkets went to the trouble and expense of bringing in a lot of fresh fish, so this simple message—FRESH FISH—was a viable USP. They also, incidentally, were getting the right message to the right market; most of Stew Leonard's customers were upscale consumers with the money to buy fresh fish, the time and inclination to prepare a meal with it, and an appreciation for it. Still, something was wrong. The fresh fish wasn't flying out of its display case. Why? It turned out to be a presentation problem.

One of their customers told them that she wished they had real fresh fish, like the fish at the wharfside fish markets. Of course, Leonard's did, but it didn't look like it. The fresh fish at the dockside markets was lying there unpackaged, on slabs of ice. So Stew Leonard's people divided the fresh fish that came in each day and presented the same fish two different ways: one, as they had been, cleaned up and nicely packaged; two, unpackaged, on a slab of ice, in a little display unit topped with a sign reading Fresh Fish Market.

Guess what? Their sales of fresh fish more than doubled.

In 1983, I began coaching chiropractors on marketing and sales, and quickly determined that the chiropractors who wore white doctor coats and even kept a stethoscope hanging around their necks (despite the fact that chiropractors have no use for it) and put their staffs in medical-looking uniforms were significantly more successful than chiropractors who dressed in jacket and tie only or even more casually, and permitted staffs to dress as they pleased. We measured their success by charting their rate at converting prospective patients to paid patients, the size and growth of the practice, the number of referrals, their fee levels, and their total income. I have not wavered on this point and today counsel these chiropractors and other professionals to present themselves "packaged" in the most reassuring way possible, considering peoples' expectations. In advertising, we never use a photo of a doctor not dressed as a doctor.

Very recently, I consulted with a company selling a rather high-priced personal care product to women by means of print advertising and direct mail driving them to call and then be sold to by telephone sales agents, with the product then shipped by Priority Mail. They came to me with a shockingly high return-for-refund rate, which can be fatal to a direct marketing company. There was no reason for customers to be dissatisfied with the product, and most of the returns were of a still sealed, unused product. The problem was glaringly obvious. Presentation. The product was shipped in a plain brown box with a plain-Jane, black-and-white label; took three to seven days to arrive thanks to the vagaries of Priority Mail; and the inside was presented very plainly, labeled plainly, and absent any postpurchase reassurance. By changing to a more impressive-looking box, using three-day Federal Express, more elegant interior packaging, and adding both a letter and a DVD reselling the virtues of the product, we slashed refunds nearly in half and recaptured enormous sums, or to put it another way, increased net sales by about 30 percent.

There are many places that poor presentation can hurt you: in advance of the first sale to the customer, in your advertising and marketing; at point of sale, in your store or office or your or your salesperson's dress, comportment, language; or after the sale, in the reinforcement and reassurance of the customer. There are three experiences in which marketing messages are at work: before the sale/purchase, during the sale/purchase itself, and after the sale/purchase. We're going to focus here on everything leading up to the sale, but you should carefully examine and watch over all three.

ULTIMATE MARKETING SECRET WEAPON #2:
Being Clearly Understood

One of the worst presentation mistakes is confusion. That's what happens when what seems clear to you isn't clear to others. It wasn't clear to the grocery shoppers that the fresh fish was really fresh; the grocer thought saying so made it so. It wasn't clear to the women receiving the high-priced personal care product that it was of elite, luxury quality and its ingredients superior to all others because it didn't look right based on their preconceived ideas of how such a product should be presented to them. Many advertising campaigns and marketing materials and even face-to-face selling scripts err in the same way. They fail to clearly communicate.

Presentation Key #1: Be Well Organized

The customer has to be led up **five steps to a buying or action decision** —to return an order form, redeem a coupon, call for an appointment, come into a store, or buy a product or service—and the five steps are the same for any and every product or service, for marketing to consumers or business-to-business:

- Step 1: Awareness of need and/or desire
- Step 2: Picking the "thing" that fulfills the need/desire
- Step 3: Picking the source for the thing
- Step 4: Accepting the source's price/value argument
- Step 5: Finding reasons to act now

Sometimes you have to start your presentation at step 1; other times you get to start on step 2. A company selling dog food gets to start on step 2; a company selling dog vitamins has to start on step 1. This decision about where to start your presentation is an important one.

Go back to the Yellow Pages and again turn to the ads in your section (or visit the websites you visited before) and, of course, examine your own marketing materials. Ask yourself whether or not, from the headline on down, the ads present their messages according to the organized structure above.

I think you'll agree with me—most do not. Believe me, this is a big mistake. Every presentation of a marketing message via any and every medium should adhere to a safe, proven, effective structure.

Let me give you a couple of great examples of this structure in action.

Example #1

For many years, as I said, I did a considerable amount of consulting work within the chiropractic profession, helping practitioners learn to market their services effectively. I consider the members of this profession my friends, but I must tell you that they remain stubbornly lousy at marketing. Most of them deviate from this organized structure in most of the media they use, yet they need to follow these five steps as precisely as any marketer I can think of.

For them, step 1 has to be creating awareness of the need or the desire: reminding people that they suffer chronically from, say, headaches or low back pain or neck stiffness, that they consume frightening quantities of pills, drugs, and alcohol to mute the symptoms, and that deep down inside they desire optimum health and fitness. Chiropractors *cannot* afford to assume that the public is instantly, automatically interested in this.

ULTIMATE MARKETING SECRET WEAPON #3:
Carefully and Thoroughly Eliminate All Assumptions

Step 2, then, and only then, is to present chiropractic as a viable, effective, accepted, credible, safe, gentle, nonsurgical, nondrug alternative treatment for various problems and ailments. Step 3, only after completing steps 1 and 2, is the individual chiropractor presenting his USP-empowered marketing message and offer.

Much of chiropractic advertising and marketing sabotages itself by beginning with step 3.

Example #2

A client I mentioned earlier in this book, a group of financial advisors specializing in working with trailing-edge boomers and seniors, has to carefully follow these five steps to achieve the best results. In getting a prospective new client to step forward and ask (i.e., grant permission) for the agent to begin discussions about this person's private financial affairs and needs, that agent must first (step 1) make the senior very aware (and anxious about) hazards and potential losses he may face because of information he does not know and is not being given by the government or his regular accountant. "Shocking" and upsetting facts are used to create this awareness. Here are samples of the bullet points in the marketing messages used by these advisors when offering a free seminar or a free book.

DISCOVER:

1. Exactly How Obama's Health Care Plan Affects YOU:
   What You Need to Know About the 2,000-Page Obamacare Bill! YOUR ABILITY TO GET THE CARE YOU NEED DEPENDS ON FACTS ABOUT THIS the media is NOT telling you.
2. How to tap into little-known gov't money to pay nursing-home bills.
3. How <u>VETERANS can get $1,949.00 PER MONTH</u>, TAX-FREE, to pay for long-term care.
   It's CRIMINAL that Veterans aren't better informed of benefits they deserve!
4. How to protect your home and savings from new, nasty "medical taxes."
5. <u>WARNING:</u> Illness, need for care for one spouse can STEAL THE COUPLE'S HOME and drain their savings—but this danger can be avoided with proper advance planning!
6. <u>WARNING:</u> Why your life insurance may be a "sitting duck" for taxes—and how to fix it.

7. <u>WARNING:</u> The Hidden Mistake Made with Revocable Trusts—that traps your money.
Insurance salesmen SELL insurance, lawyers SELL trusts—but most people do NOT fully understand what they buy!

8. <u>"Call To Action":</u> It's YOUR money, they're YOUR benefits, YOU worked hard and did the right things your whole life—do NOT let any of your just rewards and financial security be stolen away from you just because of a financial planning, insurance, or investment mistake!

9. <u>EXTRA WARNING:</u> If you have over $250,000.00 of invested/investable assets OR are currently invested in MUTUAL FUNDS, there is CRITICAL INFORMATION you need to know!
Tax traps, hidden charges, hidden fees—mutual funds are a "minefield"! YOUR MONEY COULD DO BETTER & BE BETTER PROTECTED FROM THE VOLATILE, DANGEROUS STOCK MARKET—for which many experts including Rubini and Dent are predicting a COMING CRASH to a Dow of 5,000.

10. <u>THE TRUTH ABOUT GOLD:</u> You see the TV ads, hear the radio ads . . . on Beck, Limbaugh, FOX, CNBC, etc.—what MUST you know BEFORE you buy gold or if you already own it . . . that "They" won't tell you!

Many advisors who advertise, offer seminars, or use direct mail to solicit appointments skip to step 2 or, worse, step 3. They begin by talking about financial products and services or, even worse, about themselves—but in doing so, they're often talking to deaf ears, because their prospects are not aware there's anything to be worried about with the way they have their affairs arranged now or think they've "heard all this before." These prospects are besieged by insurance salespeople, financial planners, investment advisors, banks, etc., trying to sell them insurance, annuities, living trusts, and estate plans. More of that pushing of product is just clutter. With the advisors I develop marketing for and coach, I back them up to step 1 each and every time they advertise, market, promote, present, or sell.

How to Create Alarm or Need

"What is *alarm?* The sight of blood. A phone call in the middle of the night. Shooting chest pains. Losing sight of your child in a crowd . . . alarm has a unique ability to compel people to do things they otherwise don't care to do, in order to avoid consequences . . . the more clearly a message points to consequences, the more urgently people focus on the message."—Sally Hogshead, author, *Fascinate*

Presentation Key #2: Ignite Interest

I don't care if you are marketing Hostess Twinkies, garden hoses, industrial widgets, or any one of a zillion commodities or services that you and everyone you know has accepted as dull and ordinary and mundane, maybe even trivial. There is a way, and you *must* find it, to present that message in a truly interesting manner.

> ### ULTIMATE MARKETING SIN #1:
> ### Being Boring

Some years back, I did some consulting work for a manufacturer of security cameras and video monitoring devices for retail stores. I'm here to tell you that there's nothing inherently fascinating about this. Still, I knew that I had to *ignite interest* in the store owner's mind and heart, intellectually and emotionally. I invented a giveaway booklet with this obviously provocative title:

HOW TO STEAL YOUR BOSS BLIND!
AN EMPLOYEE'S GUIDE TO GETTING WHAT'S COMING TO YOU

Believe me, when a store owner saw this book, his interest *was* ignited. He eagerly, passionately wanted to know what was in the book.

The Power of Secrets

The word "secret" evokes a powerful emotional response in most people. It instantly hits our curiosity button. For some reason, just as cats are bothered by closed doors, we are driven nuts by secrets. We want to know. You can ignite interest easily if you have secrets to divulge. Consider this: Would you be interested, or do you know somebody who would be interested, in knowing **a medical doctor's secret** for absolutely, 100 percent suppressing hunger so you can diet, even skip meals or fast with no hunger pains, no desire for food? If I told you that this doctor's secret had been tested and proven on 1,000 patients, would that make it even more interesting to you? What if this secret had, up until now, been kept for only the doctors themselves and privileged patients like movie stars, but finally, someone was going public with this incredible discovery? You can see the power of secrets.

When marketing this retail theft-control service, we had a very dramatic story to tell. My client was a reformed deliveryman-thief who conspired with store employees and stole merchandise and money from virtually every store on his delivery route. To store owners' surprise, he was the norm, not the exception. In the supermarket, convenience store, and drug store industry, employee and deliveryman theft is triple the amount of losses to shoplifting, and it is epidemic. Those are facts, but facts alone are surprisingly uninteresting even where there is money or health or hazard involved. But in my client, we had a real villain with true confessions to reveal. We had an opportunity for a dramatic presentation.

You may or may not have an inherently as dramatic a story, but you need to wrack your brain for the germ of one that can be embellished. I find many clients have such assets that they do not consider important. One client, a health care products company selling to seniors at over 1,000 offices, had, as its still-living founder, a bona fide World War II hero—a fighter pilot shot down and escaped from behind enemy lines, an Audie Murphy/John Wayne figure. Buying their product required a senior man to set ego aside and do something he felt "unmanly" doing. Someone had to speak for this company in a marketing message that made it okay for a tough guy to buy the product, even make buying it a courageous and heroic thing to do. They had the perfect spokesperson for this message and weren't using him!

If at all possible, you should **find ways to add drama to your presentations**. I've done a lot of script writing and consulting work in the TV infomercial business—those thirty-minute-long commercials that look like TV shows—and I admire the kind I've had little to do with: those that feature dramatic demonstrations. Maybe you remember one of the classics in the *Amazing Discoveries* series of infomercials, selling car polish, where they set fire to the hood of the car and poured acid on it! Or Ron Popeil's Food Dehydrator. Or the vacuum cleaner with suction so strong it can pick up a bowling ball. I've had to work on much more difficult infomercials, often featuring interviews and conversations. When the product can be the star, it's an advantage.

You can make the presentation of your marketing message more interesting in many different ways, some depending on the medium being used, including:

1. Dramatic first-person story—the person behind the product
2. Before/after photographs
3. Dramatic stories of satisfied customers
4. Shocking statistics and revelations (if you can show any controversy, all the better)
5. Dramatic slogans, headlines, statements
6. Physical demonstrations

Presentation Key #3: Ask for Action

Most marketing-message presentations are too wimpy. They stop short of demanding any action. They may communicate "Here's our beautiful new car," but they stop short of saying "Get into a showroom this weekend, take a test drive, and take home a free case of Coca-Cola just for test-driving it." Or they may say "Here's our wonderful new shampoo," but they stop short of saying "Now go to your phone, dial our toll-free number, or go to our website and we'll rush you a free sample and $5.00 in discount coupons."

> **ULTIMATE MARKETING SECRET WEAPON #4:**
> **The Guts to Ask for Action Every Time, in Every Presentation**

Very early in my selling career, I heard the great sales and motivation speaker Zig Ziglar say that **the difference between being a professional salesperson and a professional *visitor* is asking for the order.** Zig also said: "Timid salespeople have skinny kids." I, fortunately, accepted this idea and have never, ever been shy about asking for the action. However, most salespeople, even otherwise very good ones, are held back by this hesitancy, hobbled by some strange love of subtlety. This same timidity carries over into dumb, non-direct-response advertising and feckless marketing. Why be shy about purpose?

Later in life, I had the privilege of appearing on the same seminar tour with Zig over 200 times. I never once saw him speak without asking for the order.

Once I spent a full week touring one company's real-estate developments, pretending to be a prospective buyer and putting the salespeople through their paces. Almost without exception, all the salespeople did a fine job of establishing rapport, being courteous and friendly, asking smart questions, and showing me the communities and the houses. And, almost unanimously, they all stopped way short of asking me to buy.

Four chiropractors joined together and manned a very attractive, professional-appearing booth at a health fair in a busy shopping mall over Labor Day weekend but wound up with no new patients from their efforts. Care to know why? They never asked anybody to book an exam appointment. They smiled, greeted, handed out literature, gave scoliosis exams, checked blood pressure, and answered questions, but they never asked anybody to take any action.

Read This Book!

Bill Glazer was one of the relatively rare small-business owners who really, really, really gets marketing, and he transformed his menswear business into a marketing business. The goods became secondary, the marketing everything, and his stores' sales and profits soared. Ultimately, more than 5,000 retailers nationwide became members of Bill's group and used his advertising. For every business owner, he wrote the book *Outrageous Advertising That's Outrageously Successful,* which I highly recommend.

The president of Glazer-Kennedy Insider's Circle™, Bill Glazer, now a celebrated advertising guru, formerly owned and operated his own menswear stores. He was initially a student of my work and would build a new Ultimate Marketing Plan for his stores each year. One of the great things about all the advertising and marketing Bill did for his stores is that he never failed to ask for specific action—and he asked a lot. Following, you'll see the last page of a multipage mailer sent to his retail stores' customers. Note how many times he asks for action—I've numbered them by hand for you. Six times on one page! This is the way to do it.

Listen: If you can't attend during the 4-days mentioned above, you can still come into either store on Monday, July 5th or Tuesday, July 6th and enter our gift certificate drawing. Either way...

(1)
YOU'LL GET SOME INCREDIBLE BARGAINS
(Just Take A Look At The Sheet Enclosed)

WARNING: If you plan to buy new clothes anytime this year, you owe it to yourself to attend and take advantage of this special preferred client only offer. Take good care of this letter and we'll look forward to seeing you sometime Thursday through Sunday. (2)

Sincerely, (3)

Bill Glazer

Bill Glazer (4)
Owner

Present This Letter and Receive a...
SURPRISE FREE GIFT
Gage With this letter. Valid July 1-4, 2004 only.
While supplies last.
SKU# 33-610

P.S. **DON'T FORGET:** This special savings event is good for 4-DAYS ONLY, this coming Thursday through Sunday (both stores open Sunday, July 4th from 11am-5pm).

PLUS, THIS LETTER ENTITLES YOU TO:

• A surprise **FREE** gift
• Automatically enters you in our drawing for a chance to win a $250 **GAGE GIFT CERTIFICATE.** (Gage "World Class" Menswear employees are not eligible to win Gift Certificate contest. No purchase is necessary. You need not be present to win.)
• An **EXTRA 10% OFF** your purchases even on our 'Rock Bottom' Final Reductions merchandise when you present this letter between July 1-4, 2004 (6)

(5) **BRING A FRIEND IF YOU WISH!**

Present This Letter and Receive an...
EXTRA 10% Off
All Final Reduction Merchandise
Gage With this letter. Valid July 1-4, 2004 only.
Not valid with any other offer.
SKU# 33-609

Gage
SINCE 1946
Baltimore's World Class Men's Stores
www.gagemenswear.com

Downtown - 200 W. Baltimore St.   Owings Mills - 9616 Reisterstown Rd.
Across from 1st Mariner Arena   Owings Mills in Valley Centre
410-727-0763   **410-581-5351**
Mon.-Sat. 9 to 6 & Sunday 11 to 4   *Mon.-Sat. 10 to 9 & Sunday 12 to 5*
Free Parking at Arrow Garage

Join our Repeat Rewards Program and save every time you shop!

Touch Base Every Time

You don't have to be a baseball fan to know this rule: Even when the hitter whacks the ball out of the ballpark, it's not a home run on the scoreboard until he goes around the bases—and touches every one. In gym class baseball I was tagged out after hitting a home run and walking the bases because I carelessly stepped over second base instead of on it. I've never forgotten that.

The right presentation of the right marketing message touches every base, every time. It assumes nothing. It takes nothing for granted.

A good presentation strives for clarity and simplicity and even, many times, brevity—but never, ever achieves those things through shortcuts or skipping bases.

Targets

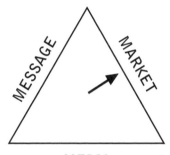

MEDIA

There is an old joke about a wife insisting on joining her husband for the first time on his annual deer hunting trip. He stations her at the bottom of the hill, instructs her to fire her gun in the air if she sees any deer—which is very unlikely at that location—and he and his buddy stomp off into the woods. Shortly thereafter, they hear shots and run back through the woods and down the hill to find the wife holding a gun on a very unhappy looking fellow. "Okay, lady," he says, "it's your deer. Can I at least get my saddle off of it?"

Obviously, no matter how well equipped you are with the best gun, bullets, and other hunting equipment, you still won't do very well aiming at the wrong targets.

ULTIMATE MARKETING SIN #2:
Wasting Your Weaponry Aiming at the Wrong Targets

My friend and true marketing guru, the late, great Gary Halbert, posed this question: "If you were going to open a new hamburger stand in town, and you could have any one asset or advantage, what is the one thing you would want most?"

Many people answer the best hamburgers in town, or a secret sauce, or a great cook, or a commanding name, logo, or character, like Ronald McDonald, or a huge bankroll for a major advertising campaign. But Gary's answer was: *a starving crowd.* Success factor #3 is a starving crowd or the close equivalent—highly motivated, highly responsive customers—for your products, services, or business. It is my contention this is paramount, above all else, more important than all other factors.

Learning the Lesson

My first introduction to the idea of targeted marketing was so strange that I've never forgotten it, and the more I've learned about the idea, the more I've appreciated that early lesson.

A man with zero training in marketing was running a direct-sales company, selling distributorships for his products at $5,000.00 each. His system was to send out a fairly expensive direct-mail package, get back inquiries, and turn those over to staff salespeople called "recruiters," who then phoned or visited the prospective distributors and tried to get them to attend a group meeting. As you can see, this process adds up to a sizeable investment in each prospect. And, for a while, he was literally mailing to the White Pages—to everybody and anybody. He knew this was incredibly inefficient, but he had no idea how to do it differently. One day, he took notice of the odd fact that a huge majority of his successful distributors had crew cuts. This was in the late sixties and crew cuts were supposedly "out." But *his* guys with crew cuts were stubborn individualists, about forty to fifty years old, living in small towns and working in blue-collar jobs—truck drivers, policemen, high school coaches.

To his credit, he didn't just take notice of this odd fact. He acted on it. He sent his recruiters out to barber shops all over the state and bought the names, addresses, and telephone numbers of their customers with crew cuts! His success rate with these grade-A prospects was phenomenal.

When he first told me about this, about twenty years ago, I laughed at him. The whole thing sounded ridiculous to me. Maybe it just did to you, too. But now, with 20/20 hindsight, I can tell you that he had stumbled on to the essence of brilliant marketing. He had found one of the three means of picking the right targets: **demographics.**

This Is for You, Too

Every **product,** *every* **service,** *every* **business either appeals or has the potential to appeal much more strongly to a certain definable group of people than it appeals to *all* people.**

Despite this fact, most marketers get to their grade-A prospects only by lucky accident—by throwing out their message to everybody and letting the right people find it. This is like getting a message to your aunt in Pittsburgh by dropping 100,000 copies of your letter out of an airplane as you fly over Pennsylvania. I call this "blind archery." Blindfolded, given an unlimited supply of arrows, and some degree of luck, you'll hit the target eventually. And you will hit it once out of every *x* times you shoot off an arrow. Of course, you'll also hit innocent bystanders, bushes, fence posts, stray animals, and everything else around.

And arrows are one thing. Dollars are another. Nobody has an unlimited supply of dollars to play with. For a time, in boom years, there was so much money sloshing around and so many people spending so freely on so many things, many business owners got away with playing blind archery with their marketing. The costly waste and inefficiency was concealed by sales and profits that were more than satisfactory. Super-investor Warren Buffet is widely credited with the quote: "You can't see who's naked until the tide goes out." And that's what happened. The recession arrived and the consumer spending tide went out, and a lot of business leaders were shocked by their own nakedness as well as others'. Today, the cost of gross inefficiency in marketing is unaffordable and dangerous. No business is safe from the damage brought on by untargeted marketing.

Conversely, any and every business, from the tiniest to the largest, can convert to efficient targeted marketing. There is some way for every business to determine who is a "best customer" and then to focus resources on reaching out to and for those exact customers. If you have the will to do it, you can find a way to do it.

A Few Examples of Targeted Marketing in Action

Example #1

A fellow in the carpet-cleaning business told me that direct mail never paid off for him. When we investigated the area he had mailed to, we found a very high percentage of renters. Over 70 percent were tenants, not homeowners. "How'd you pick this area, anyway?" I asked him.

"It was the same zip code as my office," he answered.

"Ever drive it, like you were shopping for a home?"

"Nope," he admitted.

"Let's go," I said, and off we went, driving up and down about thirty streets in the area for a couple of hours. We saw many homes in desperate need of repair or paint, poorly maintained lawns, and cars in the driveways and carports five years old or older, some up on jacks being fixed.

"Based on what we've seen outside, who would you expect to see inside these houses?" I asked. 'Nuff said.

The antidote to this direct-mail failure was not fixing the literature; it was simply selecting a better target. The carpet-cleaning guy spent the next few days driving the neighborhoods in various zip codes surrounding his office until he found one where the homes shouted pride of ownership.

In the first area, his mailing had pulled less than one-fourth of 1 percent in response. Mailing to residents in the new area, the same mailing pulled over 2½ percent.

Now, get this: this wasn't so much a demographic distinction as a psychographic one. The neighborhoods he wound up mailing to successfully did not have significantly higher priced or more valuable homes; the residents weren't of different age, education, or affluence. In terms of raw demographics, the winners and losers were about the same. The difference was in their *attitude* about their homes. Pride of ownership is a mindset, not a demographic statistic. This is important because it is very likely that your best customers share a mindset, philosophy, way of thinking, or habitual behavior that makes them especially receptive to you and your products or services.

Example #2

Many of my clients in very different businesses have discovered the power and leverage of properly targeted marketing. One, in a rather curious business, ran a foreign brides brokerage, helping frustrated American men meet and marry women from dozens of different foreign countries. Others in this unusual field typically advertise and sell directories or memberships to websites where the women themselves advertise and the men shop. But he provided a comprehensive match-making service at significant fees, and needed clients who were quite serious about their goal of finding and marrying an imported wife and who were able and willing to pay substantial fees to do so.

Historically, he did all of his advertising in general publications, like *USA Today*. At one of my group coaching meetings, I asked him who his clients were. He initially said, "Just about everybody," and named ministers, salespeople, business owners, truck drivers, and doctors. Pushed hard by me and others in the group, he went home and closely examined his records and found that over 50 percent of his clients were twice-divorced, long-haul truck drivers. Over half! This quickly led to a dramatic change in allocation of ad dollars, focusing on targeted media like truck drivers' magazines, his own "magalog" distributed in free take-one racks placed in truck stops, and other niche media. Profits soared!

Example #3

Where did founder Tom Monaghan open up his early Domino's Pizza locations? In college towns, near college campuses. Why? Who do you know who eats pizza more often than college kids? Also, smoking the funny weed was immensely popular among college kids, and in case you don't know it, marijuana makes people very, very, very hungry, in desperate and urgent need of lots of carbs, and unable to go out and get them. I have no idea whether or not Tom thought through that, and if he did, I doubt he'd admit it, but he's a bright guy, so you decide for yourself. The point is that, quite literally, he found a starving crowd.

The Three Best Ways to Target Market

The first and most commonly used target marketing is **geographic targeting**, just like my friend in the carpet-cleaning business did. Most businesses that need their customers to come to their store or office or that need to schedule appointments and send salespeople out obviously need to restrict the geography of their marketing. They advertise only in the local newspaper or shopper, use coupon decks mailed to their own or adjacent zip codes, and target direct mailers to those same zips. Relatively recently, it became possible and practical to use the Internet—the *world wide* web—to advertise local businesses to local consumers, too.

There's nothing wrong and many things right with this. If you've never read Russell Conwell's classic book *Acres of Diamonds* or heard Earl Nightingale's great recorded message "Greener Pastures," you should; you'll gain new appreciation for the "value" awaiting discovery right in your own backyard. Nothing wrong with the backyard at all. In fact, many businesses neglect it for no good reason whatsoever.

However, I suggest keeping three things in mind when you are going to select your target markets via geographical considerations:

1. Make Sure That the Apparent *Nature* of the People Living There Works for You

This is a cheap (in fact, free) and very simplistic look at demographics, but it is nonetheless effective. Do what my carpet-cleaning entrepreneur and I did: drive the neighborhoods. Look around and get a feel for the people who live there. You can tell a lot just by driving around. What does the condition of the homes and yards tell you? What kinds of cars predominate? If compacts and sporty cars, think young marrieds. If big sedans and luxury cars, assume middle-aged. Do you see a lot of tricycles and skateboards, or a lot of basketball backboards on the garages? You may very well be able to choose preferable neighborhoods or zip code areas this way. You may also discover things that will cause you to modify your themes, copy, and offers.

Whether your geographic market is local, regional, certain states, all across the country but only the small towns, or whatever, within it there are divisions or "clumps" of different kinds of customers. You *want* to rule out hunks of any geographic area you're marketing in. You *want* to be able to skip streets or blocks or neighborhoods or apartment buildings or entire zip codes. You *want* to reduce the size of your prospect universe so that you are using your resources efficiently and can spend more on each "best" prospect because you are spending less, little, or nothing on bad prospects.

Get this: Your net profits from marketing will be determined more by your diligence with this discriminatory selection of prospects than by anything else.

2. Once You Find a Geographic Target Market That Works for You, Work It to Death

Dominate it. People in the real-estate business use the term "farming." When a real-estate agent farms an area, he strives to become its best-known and loved agent. He mails to every homeowner in the area, goes around door to door and introduces himself, distributes a monthly newsletter, sends holiday greeting cards, even gets creatively involved with the community: giving away free pumpkins at Halloween, sponsoring a neighborhood block party and swap meet, and so on. It's a lot of work, but it's smart work. If you get adept at using media, particularly direct mail, you can replace much or even all of the manual labor stuff.

There's no reason any retail or service business can't follow this example. If I had a florist shop, a restaurant, or a car wash, I could do exactly the same thing in a targeted residential or business neighborhood. I would frequently mail to everybody. I would take an hour each day and go out and personally introduce myself to the neighbors. I would send holiday greetings. I would throw a party. I would lead a charitable effort in the area for a worthwhile group.

A second selection method has to do with demographics. Demographics are the statistical and behavioral things given groups of people have in common. Demographic selection can be as simple as targeting a preferred age group or as complex as targeting women age thirty-five to forty-five who have careers, read both the *Wall Street Journal* and *Cosmopolitan,* carry the American Express card, travel by air at least three times a year, and buy clothes by mail order or online.

Every medium has and can provide detailed demographic information about its readers, listeners, viewers, or customers. While some media's data are more reliable than others, most are pretty accurate—the media need this same data to make good editorial, programming, or product selections. You can and should take this information very seriously when making media decisions.

If you're renting mailing lists, the same kind of data is available for most lists. More significantly, you can "merge-purge" two or more lists together to get exactly the prospective customers you want. It can be quite costly to do sophisticated merge-purges, but even so it's usually a bargain compared to the costly waste of playing blind archery with direct mail.

I'm often asked about lists—how do I find the names of my ideal prospects? Well, good news: privacy is dead. There are compiled demographic lists, built from publicly available data, using home ownership, age, marital status, household income, net worth, education, occupations, and similar factors to assemble specific prospect groups out of any geography. Of more certain value, there are response lists, usually offering the same demographic breakouts, but also made up of known responders, inquirers, buyers, subscribers, or donors. Just for example, last I looked, you can rent the Society for the Prevention of Cruelty for Animals list of 260,000+ donors, sorted by donation amount, frequency of donation, gender, age, and geography. As many undoubtedly own pets, a local pet store or a national pet products catalog company might find portions or even the entirety of this list productive. But so might a local bookstore promoting a book signing with an author of a book about dogs.

List research is best conducted yourself, painstakingly, at *www .SRDS.com*. It is not as easy as just calling a local list broker and leaving it up to them, unless all you want is a demographic list compiled from public data. You can also find demographic lists online at *www.Info USA.com*. But if you're going after response lists, go to SRDS.com.

A few warnings: First of all, this is more complicated than most small-business owners have the stomach for. I can't help that. If you refuse to engage in smart and sophisticated marketing work because it is difficult or difficult to understand at first, I have neither great advice nor sympathy for you. Small income and long-standing frustration with small income is the deserved reward for insisting on having an easy-button or doing nothing at all.

Second, if you're a small, local business, when you go into the list rental marketplace, you're going to bump up against minimums of 5,000 names or more. And if you're looking for something from, say, the Artichokes of the Month Club list, there won't be 5,000 or maybe even 1,000 in your little community. You may have to rent 5,000 but will only be able to use 460, unless you can get owners of a business like your gourmet shop that stocks 600 varieties of pickled vegetables in other cities to go in with you on the list rental. But let's say you rent that list at $75.00 per 1,000 x 5 = $375.00, and you can only use 460 names on it. They cost you, then, $.82 each. If you can only use 46, they cost you $8.20 each. Exactly how else are you going to find the 460 or 46 passionately committed artichoke freaks in your area? And how much will you spend with mass advertising trying to flush them out of the woodwork?

Third, don't rule out this kind of highly targeted direct mail, even if you're trying to do business online and be an e-commerce merchant. One of my richest clients at the time I'm writing this book mails postcards that I wrote for him to rented lists of buyers and subscribers of a certain sort, driving them to a website to see a video sales presentation and buy a product. This year, he'll mail over 1 million of those postcards.

A Few Examples of Commercially Available Lists

Al Franken For Senate Donors (40,029)
American Driver Auto Insurance Buyers—By Insurance Co. (6 million)
Buyers or inquirers re. cruise vacations (540,000)
Pay-Day Loan Applicants (1.2 million)
Holiday Cookbook Buyers (287,000)
Boat & Yacht Owners w. Marine Radio Licenses (311,000)

Women of Faith Event Attendees (676,000)
Health Central newsletter subscribers (192,000)
Supertrax Int'l snowmobile owners (5,300)
Affinity Clubs (www.cdmlist.com):
Nat'l Health & Wellness Club (81,000)
Cooking Club of America (572,000)
Creative Home Arts Club (306,000)
History Channel Club (287,000)
Nat'l Home Gardening Club (622,000)
N. American Fishing Club (856,000)

Think again about my friend in the carpet-cleaning business. After choosing one or several zip code areas based on his drive-by observations, he could get even pickier. He might make the logical assumption that people in certain income brackets are better prospects than others. Folks with household incomes of, say, less than $30,000.00 a year might find money tight and choose to go through the agony of shampooing their own carpets to save money.

Since he accepts VISA and MasterCard, he might prefer to mail only to people who have those credit cards, and since families get their carpets dirtier more often, he might want to skip mailing to single people.

So he sits down with his list broker and says: "In these zips, I want married homeowners with kids, with household income of $30,000.00 and up, who have MasterCards or VISA cards." Using lists derived from the census, credit card holder lists, property ownership records, and other readily available sources, the broker can deliver that exact list or something very close to it.

Incidentally, it can be helpful to collect demographic data about your present customers. If you find certain biases or commonalities in your present customers, you may be able to use them in your criteria for future targeting.

If it's worth it to him, and it might very well be, he could experiment with response lists rather than compiled lists—and were he marketing to more affluent homeowners, I'd definitely suggest it. *Martha Stewart Living* subscribers or buyers of books on entertaining at home, active customers of a home furnishings catalog, or buyers of kitchen gadgets might be productive, as it seems they are "about" their home and home life.

3. Market by Affinity or Association

I like this approach and use it a great deal for myself and my clients. Let me give you a personal example: For many years, beginning in 1978, I was a member of the National Speakers Association, one of two trade associations for lecturers and seminar leaders. I went out of my way to be visible in the association, through a variety of means, and for a number of years I believe my name recognition was at about 70 to 80 percent of the total membership, about 4,000 people at the time. Those 4,000 people and I had much in common: First, obviously, I knew them and, more important, they knew me. I could call attention to our affinity by addressing them as "colleagues" and "fellow members." We shared the same business activities, experiences, concerns, and problems. Because I was a known, respected success in the field, the members were interested in what I had to say and in whatever I recommended.

In the time I treated this as a target market, I sold millions of dollars of goods and services to its members. Some years, as much as one-third of my income was derived from this very small market. I was occasionally able to reap pure passive income simply from licensing my endorsement to someone else's product or service being offered to this very small market.

Geographically, these people were scattered all over the United States, Canada, and several foreign countries. Demographically, they had few, if any, dominant commonalties. They were men, women, young, old, fat, thin, conservative, liberal, rich, poor, married, single, with families, without families. But they were still a perfect target market for me purely because of our mutual association. Because of affinity.

As evidence of how well affinity worked for me with this target market, back when I was doing revisions and updating the second edition of this book, I was in the midst of a direct-mail campaign to this list for a new product and had brought in $226,400.00. Just a year before that, I had conducted a simple direct-mail campaign for another new information product to this group and did nearly $600,000.00 in sales. All from only about 4,000 people.

I've since moved on, and our own Glazer-Kennedy Insider's Circle™ organization is much larger than the National Speakers Association and has become, in essence, my home market. There is also the linked, more specialized Information Marketing Association. From these markets come much of my present-day consulting, copywriting, and coaching clients; the few speaking engagements I care to do; and an ample number of other opportunities.

Many other businesspeople can apply this same principle to their trade or professional associations or to the chamber of commerce, Toastmasters, Jaycees, other business and civic groups, church groups, PTAs—whatever they belong to. I encourage chiropractors and dentists I consult with, for example, to get out of their offices at least eight hours a week to join and actively participate in a number of these associative target markets. Then, instead of advertising to a neighborhood, they can advertise to their fellow members. Instead of farming a community, they can farm a fraternity.

ULTIMATE MARKETING SECRET WEAPON #5: Tailoring and Delivering Your Message to the Right Target

I find the pizza wars endlessly interesting. Domino's took the industry by storm by focusing on delivery, initially to an identifiable, identified starving crowd. Those the chain was after knew it was for them. My friend, Gene Landrum, author of an excellent series of books on the psyche of the entrepreneur, was a creator of the enormously successful Chuck E. Cheese pizza chain, which is all about kids and game playing. Our famous Glazer-Kennedy Insider Circle™ Member Diana Coutu has made her pizza business all about—imagine this!—the pizza, unabashedly charging premium prices for premium pizza. All three could coexist and prosper on the same street, within eyesight of each other, because each is about something different; each is for a different customer.

In Las Vegas, for many years most casino-hotels aggressively pursued the business of the high rollers. An acquaintance of mine has the title Casino Host at one of the biggest hotels on the Strip. He's actually a recruiter who goes to other hotels, to parties in Beverly Hills and New York where the rich gather, even to Japan, to invite and inveigle high rollers to come to the hotel he represents. When they do, they are his honored and privileged guests, with complimentary rooms, meals, shows, airfare, limousines, even escorts if desired. Every big casino operation has such people. One high roller I know described Las Vegas as "the home of the $10,000.00 free drink."

Bob Stupak, mentioned earlier, ignored this market almost entirely. Nothing he did was targeted at the high roller. To the contrary, his market was middle-income, middle America, mom-and-pop, everyday folks, many of them first-time visitors to Glitter City. While the others chased the Saks customer, Bob preferred Sears. If the other hotels got people with Mercedes and even Rolls-Royces in their garages, Bob attracted the people with three-year-old minivans. While the other hotels pursued the country-club crowd, Bob recruited at the bowling alleys. For a handful of recent years, Las Vegas refocused its sights on families, with many casino resorts creating Disneyesque, family-friendly environments, and the city briefly surpassed Orlando as the number one vacation destination. However, in the post–9/11 world, the realization set in that adult customers were more reliable and valuable, so Vegas shifted back to Sin

City, with nightclubs featuring scantily clad dancers, more "skin" shows, and the suggestive ad slogan: What Happens in Vegas, Stays in Vegas. The more recent recession has been very challenging for Las Vegas. This city's business leaders are constantly, closely analyzing their different markets and constituencies, and tailoring and delivering different marketing messages to different target markets. A great deal can be gained by observing their examples.

The Profit-Boosting Secret of the NOW Buyer

In real estate, there is a thing called the "NOW buyer"—and even though the real-estate industry as a whole has been in the doldrums for a while as I write this, plenty of NOW buyers exist despite the recession, and some exist because of the recession. With **residential real estate**, these can include people who must relocate for job or family or health reasons, those with babies on the way, "Brady Bunch-ers" suddenly merging families, or somebody like Candy Spelling who had to buy her new condo as a downsizing move—it was only 17,000 square feet!—when she put her $150-million megamansion on the market. In **commercial**, it may be someone with proceeds from a real-estate or business sale that must be reinvested to avoid a tax whack, 1031 exchange buyers. In that industry, there are *personal* timing reasons that compel purchase whether the overall economy timing is good, bad, or indifferent.

In **financial services**, there are NOW buyers. They may have just inherited a substantial sum, sold a business and retired, or been a CD investor living off the fixed income from interest suddenly slashed by two-thirds that now must diversify and even take risks.

In **collectibles**, there are NOW buyers because something suddenly comes available that must be bought or lost forever. In **jewelry, vacations, and gifts**, there are NOW buyers because the tenth, twenty-fifth, and fiftieth wedding anniversaries occur only once in most peoples' lives and cannot, dare not, be ignored.

IN EVERY BUSINESS, there are must-buy-now buyers. Idiotically, most business owners make no SPECIAL attempts to identify them, find them, and sell to them differently than they sell to everyone else. Today, a must-buy-now buyer has to be worth a great deal more than any ordinary buyer who may or may not buy now but can just as easily postpone, procrastinate, or prevaricate. The marketer can and should invest considerably more in finding and wooing that must-buy-now buyer. He's worth more, so you can invest more. Since hardly anybody does, you can own an extreme competitive advantage, if you will.

Combine the must-buy-now buyer with the affluent can-buy-now buyer and you've really got something. This is demographic plus situational. Having families with family members over the age of seventy on your mailing list, if you are operating a funeral home, is smart marketing. Identifying particularly affluent families in that category is smarter. Any divorcée aged thirty-five to fifty-five is a good target for weight loss, fitness, beauty, cosmetic dentistry, and cosmetic surgery marketing, but such a divorcée of a certain level of affluence is a better target. Doesn't seem like much of a mystery to me.

The pertinent question, then, is who is *your* must-buy-now + can-buy-now buyer? The better and more complete your answer, the better able you'll be to find him.

Proof

MEDIA

The public has been lied to so much by so many that we no longer trust anybody, yet trust is needed to make most sales and to sustain most relationships. People are disillusioned and distrustful, with good reason. The hurdle is high.

There is an old joke—told to me by a very cynical businessman—about the father who puts his three-year-old son up on the fireplace mantle and holds out his hands and urges him to jump. "I'll catch you," he promises. After much coaxing and coercion, the kid jumps toward Daddy, who steps back and lets him crash to the floor. He then leans over the wailing youngster and says: "You've just learned your first great lesson of life—don't trust anybody."

The consumer and the business customers, your prospective customer or client, has been coerced off the mantle and let crash to the floor one too many times. Lucy has pulled the football away at the last minute one time too many, and Charlie Brown won't play anymore.

> ## ULTIMATE MARKETING SECRET WEAPON #6:
> ### Marketing Messages Developed with the Understanding That Recipients Will Be Stubbornly Reluctant to Believe Them

I often have clients bring me the same marketing problem: a truly irresistible offer that doesn't work.

One such client had put together the ultimate, legitimate travel premium: a certificate good for at least $500.00 worth of travel, including two nights in brand-name hotels scattered around the country, including resort locations, or a three-day Bahamas cruise for just $99.00 per person, and more. He sells these certificates to various businesses to use as premiums and incentives, at a dollar to as little as a nickel in volume—that's right!—five cents each! The recipient of the certificate needs only to pay a $10.00 processing fee to use it.

He was perplexed by the difficulty he was having getting businesses to buy and use these things. And he found that a shockingly small percentage of the people who got them make the call to redeem them. How could this be? "Why," he asked, "doesn't this work better than it does?"

By now, of course, the answer is obvious, isn't it? The darned offer is just too good to be true. People didn't believe it. In this case, it *is* obvious to you. It's a gift you'd be suspicious of if offered to you by your local auto dealer or jewelry store or restaurant. But what's *not* so obvious is that your perfectly reasonable, sensible, and legitimate offer or your truthful assertions about your product may be received with just as much suspicion.

Today, if you make any kind of a free or big-discount offer, the consumer says to himself or herself: "Who's he kidding? Nothing's free. There's got to be a catch here somewhere." Or: "Fifty percent off, my eye!

All they've done is jacked up the price so they can mark it back down. It's all baloney."

My research indicates that people don't even believe guarantees. They say: "Yeah, just try to get your money back. You've got to bring it back still wrapped in the original plastic, fill out a sixteen-part form, stand in line for three hours, and scream and yell and threaten their lives." I believe you should use, even lean heavily on, guarantees. But you have to go to extremes to make people believe them.

If you use testimonials—and I'm going to tell you that you should—they say: "I'll bet those are actors" or "I'll bet they're just made up" or "I'll bet they paid those people to say those things."

Here is the Ultimate Marketing Plan "Be Safe or Sorry" rule: Prove every single item in your case.

Prove every statement, assertion, claim, promise, offer, and warranty. Leave nothing unproven. Never presume trust or acceptance.

So, How Do We Prove Our Case?

I sat, as an uninvolved observer, in the giant, lavishly decorated law firm conference room and watched and listened as one of this country's most famous trial attorneys conducted his pretrial conference with his associates, investigators, researchers, and paralegals. Each person summarized his or her work and each gave an opinion on the probable outcome.

One young attorney assured the boss, "I think you've got enough evidence to win this thing."

The boss came unglued. He slammed his hands down on the table and rocked the room. He lunged across the table, grabbed the young guy by his Brooks Brothers lapels, yanked him up, faced him nose-tip to nose-tip, and bellowed loud enough to be heard on the opposite coast: *"Do not ever send me into a courtroom to face a jury with just enough evidence."* He paused, dropped the shocked attorney back into his chair, walked to the end of the room, and wrote these words on the blackboard:

PREPONDERANCE OF PROOF

Webster defines "preponderance" as a superiority in weight, power, importance, strength, or quantity. *Roget's Thesaurus* suggests these synonyms: majority, plurality, advantage, supremacy, maximum, lion's share, excess, surplus, redundancy, and domination. I suggest that you want all that and more when you present your case to the customer.

How to Go from Zero to Maximum Credibility

If we wanted an example of an industry with near-zero credibility, we need look no further than the people and businesses behind the automobile sitting outside in the driveway. Automobile salespeople are distrusted by everybody.

My own informal—but I think fairly accurate—survey shows that ranked at the very bottom of the trust ladder by the public are lawyers, then, still worse, politicians, then, worst of all, car salesmen. The industry has brought this on itself. Often, people in the automobile business use artificial retail prices in order to create phony discounts, advertise stripped models in order to play bait-and-switch, use deceptive sales practices, bully their customers, sell grossly overpriced insurance add-ons, and are notorious for lousy service after the sale.

Fortunately, there are good, honest exceptions to this rule. There are extremely reputable auto dealers and high-integrity auto sales professionals who must combat the negative public perception of their black-hearted brethren.

The most honest and, I think not coincidentally, the most successful automobile salesman I've ever known is Bill Glazner*, a Ford salesman in Phoenix during the years I lived there. He managed to attain maximum credibility in a business that, overall, has no credibility—a tough task, but a great marketing lesson. (* He's not to be confused with the Bill Glazer featured frequently throughout this book, publisher of my

NO B.S. MARKETING LETTER, president of Glazer-Kennedy Insider's Circle™. They are not the same person. Not related.)

For years, I bought all my cars from Bill. Here was the experience, consistent every time: When you went to buy a car from Bill, like most anywhere else, you went out on the lot and looked at cars, kicked tires, maybe test-drove a couple. Eventually you were led down the hall where the long row of salesmen's cubicles were located. These are pretty much the same everywhere. You've been in more than one. The walls are ticky-tacky plywood partitions held in place with the little screw doo-dads we had on pole lamps in the sixties. In each cubicle, there's a basic military-issue gray or green metal desk. There are two turquoise or orange plastic stackable chairs for the customers. And that is it.

Bill's cubicle was the same as the others—except for one little detail. Floor to ceiling, side to side, every square inch of wall space was covered with instant snapshots of Bill's customers, proudly posed next to their new cars, with their names and dates of purchase written on them. I never counted the photos, *but the quantity was overwhelming.* Then, if you looked a little closer, you would pick up two *patterns* in the arrangement of the snapshots. First, the relationship pattern. For example, next to the picture of me with my Lincoln, you would have seen the photo of my wife with her Taurus, my parents with their Mercury, my brother with his pickup truck, my business partner with his Lincoln, his wife with her Probe, his sales manager with his Tempo, and one of his office managers with his Escort. Also, you would have noted a historical pattern. Not just me with my current Lincoln, but backwards chronologically to me with the Lincoln before that. In some cases, there were five, even six such photos: the customer with his new car, the same customer with the car he bought several years before, again with the car he bought several years before that, again with the car he bought several years before that.

Now I'm going to tell you something that is almost unbelievable. I went there with my wife, with business associates, and with friends while they bought cars from Bill and I watched, in every case, as Bill figured up the price, wrote it on the contract, quoted the price and payment amounts, and heard the customers say, "Fine." I watched them sign on the dotted line without even once haggling over price. In the car business!

In the weight-loss business, one very successful sales representative for diet products carries a sales tool with her everywhere she goes: a photo blown up into a life-size poster of herself, fifty-four pounds heavier than she is today. She unrolls the poster and stands next to it, and the sale is made.

ULTIMATE MARKETING SECRET WEAPON #7:
Pictures That Prove Your Case

Let me tell you something funny. Bill Glazner outperformed his sales colleagues at the dealership month after month, year after year— yet he was the only salesman there with photographs up on his cubicle walls. In the diet-products company the lady with the life-size "before" poster sells for, there are over 15,000 representatives, but as far as I know only one has a life-size poster of her overweight former self.

Over four years, I built the largest integrated seminar and publishing firm exclusively teaching marketing to chiropractors and dentists, and, in one way or another, I told all of these stories to at least 15,000 doctors during those years. I'm still telling these same stories to the doctors. Yet, to the best of my knowledge, there are only a handful with a photo wall like the car salesman's.

Maybe all that is a comment on my effectiveness. I hope not. I think not. Instead, I think it is simply a reflection of the vast majority's interest in improving, but only if doing so requires no change, discomfort, or initiative. That's why, in every field, a few outearn the huge "mediocre majority" by giant margins.

Today it is very easy to incorporate photographic and video evidence into presentations on websites and other online media, and many marketers do because there is abundant evidence that doing so boosts response. But nobody should stop with what's easy. This kind of evidence should be incorporated into every media and every sales environment that is part of your business.

Who Says So?

When you make a statement, it's a claim. When your satisfied customer makes the same statement about you, that's a *fact*.

What others say about you, your company, your products, and your services is infinitely more credible than anything you can say on your own behalf.

I am here to tell you that you cannot overuse testimonials. Some businesses, notably the weight-loss industry and the skin care industry, do an outstanding job of getting and using good testimonials—watch advertising by Weight Watchers or TV infomercials, like Guthy-Renker's infomercials for Proactiv acne products or Victoria Principal skin care. After its massive recall troubles in 2010, Toyota resorted to TV commercials featuring testimonials rather than cars, and Ford quickly followed suit with a very successful campaign. This strategy will never go out of style, never run out of gas. When Priceline.com was brand new, introducing name-your-price travel purchased via the Internet, it used offline marketing and ran full-page magazine ads filled with photographs of happy Priceline customers captioned with the trips they took and the amounts of money they saved.

Testimonials are beneficial in every marketing situation, whether it's introducing yourself or a new product, service, or idea to prospects for the first time; responding to a negative situation and rebuilding trust in a marketplace; countering competition; or even reminding established customers of how happy they are. But one of the most critical needs for testimonials is in marketing the extremely unbeliev-able. A book I coauthored with Chip Kessler, *Making Them Believe*, explores the "lost marketing secrets of Dr. J. R. Brinkley," possibly the wealthiest and most controversial doctor of his time (the 1920s–1930s) who promoted goat testicle and gland transplant surgeries for men with what is now called erectile dysfunction. Long before I conceived it, Brinkley used a near clone of the entire Ultimate Marketing Plan described in this book, featuring his essential reliance on proof pro-vided by testimonials, notably including a "champion" or "poster boy" standing as dramatic proof of his promises. Here is a brief excerpt from one of Chip's chapters in the book about the doctor's most valu-able testimonial:

". . . Dr. Brinkley's paramount breakthrough, product-wise, came shortly after he moved to the town of Milford, Kansas, in 1917. Brin-kley, practicing his personal brand of herbal remedies, had hung out his shingle and patients began trickling in. One in particular, a local farmer, complained of a lack of pep in general and a loss of sexual vitality; both conditions were old Brinkley mainstays. One thing led to another and the idea was offered between physician and farmer of an instant and permanent cure by transplantation of a goat's testicles into the man's scrotum. The surgery was soon performed. A couple of weeks later, the farmer returned with the good news. Perhaps the only resident of Milford more pleased than the farmer—and maybe the farmer's wife*—was Dr. John R. Brinkley. The farmer was more than happy to spread the word and other locals soon followed onto Brinkley's operating table. A testament to the power and persuasion of a personal testimonial from the heart, and how it instantly gave Dr. Brinkley a niche that would carry him and his reputation to fame, or as others would label it, infamy.

". . . When was the last time that you made a decision or pur-chase, or took an action, and there was no doubt in your mind that you were making the right decision and moving forward on it? In your heart and mind, you knew what you were doing was right. Dr. Brinkley had this effect on people, and it made him stand head and shoulders above the average run-of-the-mill marketer, anyone else offering any product, service or cure. Most importantly, John Brinkley found ways to connect to the most profound reasons someone would want to believe in him and his proposition. A great example of this was handed to John Brinkley, but to his credit, he recognized its potential value when it occurred. John's gift came from that farmer who first went to the Milford, Kansas, physician because he lacked 'pep.' John R. Brinkley's handy-work below the belt not only brought praises from the farmer Bill Stittsworth and his wife (remember, she was so elated with her man's newly rediscovered sexual ability that she then wanted to have ovaries from a female goat transplanted herself), it also brought one other thing: Billy Stittsworth, Jr.

"There are ways of letting your target market know about the effectiveness of what product and service you are marketing . . . and then there are ways. The best is some evidence of the validity of your proposition that is intensely, profoundly motivational, triggering desire to believe. The emergence of a Stittsworth offspring not only spoke volumes about the transformative power of Brinkley's goat-glands surgery, but also tapped into the greatest desire many men and women have: the need to have a baby. For the man, it's the continuation of his name. For the woman it coincides with her need to bring life into the world. In John Brinkley's time, it was still seen as the natural, expected fulfillment of marriage, and the absence of offspring represented embarrassing failure—a sign that, either the woman was barren or the man not a man at all. A couple without at least one child was not blessed by God, and family, friends, even the entire community wondered why, and viewed them with pity. These were the cultural conditions into which Dr. Brinkley had brought his cure.

And now, Brinkley had an in-the-flesh demonstration of what a goat's transplanted testicles into a man can produce! The farmer's story and his living, breathing son provided a rock-solid foundation for others' belief. John Brinkley knew how to present his 'miracle' in a way that made people want to believe. Billy Jr. provided the unassailable reason to believe."

Resource note: Our book *Making Them Believe* is a very detailed, in-depth examination of everything that can and should be done to create belief. In addition, there is a complete home study course built around the amazing Brinkley marketing examples. Information is available at *www.ChipKessler .com*.

I'm going to let you in on a secret: As common amongst top marketers and as well-proven from the early 1900s to this day as testimonial use is, the absence or underuse of testimonials remains *the* number one marketing error I see repeated most frequently. I can promise you this: If you get nothing else out of this entire book but the inspiration to collect and heavily use as many good testimonials as you can possibly get, in as many places and ways as you can, you'll have a strong competitive advantage from that alone.

What Is a Good Testimonial?

For starters, think of a testimonial as a pair of verbal "snapshots." The first is the "Before" picture—the problem or the skepticism; the second is the "After" picture—the positive result, the pleasant surprise, the solution. "I was fat, lonely, frightened, poor, unhappy, skeptical, etc.— now, thanks to XYZ, I'm thin, popular, confident, rich, happy, and a believer!" On the following page you'll find two testimonials from our own Glazer-Kennedy Insider's Circle™ Members that have appeared in our newsletters and marketing materials, presented *exactly* like verbal Before and Afters.

PEOPLE JUST LIKE YOU DOING AMAZING THINGS WITH GKIC STYLE MARKETING

"My Use of Media Has Given Me a HUGE Jump Beyond All of My Competition"

This month's Success story:
Larry Lane, New York, NY
Lane Architecture (LaneArchitecture.net)
GOLD Member since September 2006

BEFORE GKIC:

"They do NOT teach how to bring in business in architecture school. In fact, they teach that the universe is limited and opportunities are few. The dean actually said that in order to succeed in architecture one needs to be already born into money or marry it. We were led to believe that "work will set you free" by paying your dues for many years and if you outlive your competition (like Frank Lloyd Wright did for example) you might succeed."

AFTER GKIC:

"Business opportunities started to appear after I was shown where to look, how to develop a market and message. My use of media has given me a huge jump beyond all of my competition. With the involvement of the awesome MasterMind group, I have learned how to, why to, and implemented list building, weekly radio shows, podcast, blog, newsletters, authored a book, fine-tuned a marketing plan, focused on my strengths, and become a celebrity architect. My projects have now been those I enjoy even more such as the George W Bush Presidential Library and Christies Auction House."

Glazer-Kennedy Insider's Circle™ testimonial

PROFILES IN SUCCESS

"GKIC-Philly Helped Me Achieve an ROI of 237%, IMPROVED My Marketing Presence, and Put Me in Touch with People Who Speak My Language"

Vita Borgogno, ?
Window Decorators?
Philadelphia, PA ?

Vita's Business Transformation Success Story in her own Words... ?

"I joined GKIC-Philly in July of 2008. My joining was actually a direct result of trying to cancel the GKIC Gold level membership...How GKIC handled my attempt is a testament to their marketing genius. ?

I also joined because I considered myself an astute student of marketing and especially Direct Response Marketing, having worked in a Direct Response Corporation for 7 years. So, as a business owner now, I wanted to learn more. What I didn't realize back then is that some of my learning will go way beyond incremental marketing tactics, and will encompass great mind-shifts, true inspiration, and good friends. ?

Benefits, NEW Strategies, and Improvements

➤ **Improvement #1:** Mind-shift regarding my mailings ?

"...What I didn't realize is that I can turn these direct marketing vehicles into creative, unique, action-inspiring marketing pieces that verifiably make me money. I learned dozens of very specific techniques..."?

➤ **Improvement #2:** Use of Video ?

"I've used (a flip camera) to create personal messages to my ezine-list, to supplement the Thanksgiving mailing marketing campaign, to post on the squeeze page of www.VitaV2K.com, and to add to sales pages of my products."?

➤ **Improvement #3:** The Value of Testimonials ?

"As a matter of procedure, every customer receives a thank you letter at the end of the sales cycle, along with a pre-stamped envelope and a form for their feedback"?

➤ **Improvement #4:** Resources ?

"Sometimes just one resource is all you need to save a lot of time, to make life easier, and ultimately make money. I hey range from a CD fulfillment. vendor to a 3D trinkets site. As part of GKIC-Philly, we get these resources monthly. They are specialized to the direct response industry and there would have been almost no way to obtain them otherwise..."?

➤ **Improvement #5:** Mind-shifts ?

"Marketing shifts are always welcome, naturally. But no marketing break-through can come before the mind is ready to learn about it, accept it, and embrace it. For me there are too many to list so here are two: 1) Small hinges swing big doors 2) Good is good enough"?

Glazer-Kennedy Insider's Circle™ testimonial

Second, view testimonials as strategic weapons. I suggest making two lists; one of every claim, feature, benefit, and fact about what you're marketing that you want to substantiate; second, every doubt, fear, or question that might exist in your prospective customer's mind. Then collect and use testimonials that specifically substantiate the claims that eliminate the doubts.

A Few Examples

A cafeteria wants to attract new customers. The owners are eager to emphasize the variety of foods they offer and that, unlike some cafeterias, they keep their food hot and fresh. The owners also know there are a great many people who never dream of coming to a cafeteria. Against that, they position these testimonials:

I haven't eaten in a cafeteria since high school, but I'm sure glad a friend brought me here—I'm really surprised at the tremendous variety that's offered. Finally there's someplace I can take the whole family for dinner and make everybody happy.

I've always thought that cafeteria food sat around on hot plates and got soggy. Maybe that is true elsewhere, but everything here is piping hot, fresh, and, well, really good.

A dentist "made hay" with this great testimonial:

I avoided dental care I knew I needed for almost a year because I didn't want the pain. I just couldn't stand the thought of going to the dentist. But I've got to say that Dr. Welmer and his staff were just terrific! They were patient and understanding. And things sure have changed since the last time I went to a dentist. Dr. Welmer's got the newest technology so the treatment was virtually pain-free. I was amazed.

And this powerful testimonial for a lawn service:

I'm busy, I travel a lot on business, and I hate taking care of my lawn. It always needed to be cut. Plants died. I tried different lawn care guys—you know, the guys with beat-up old pickup trucks who come around and hang Xeroxed flyers on your door, then never show up when they're supposed to. When the representative of Lawn Technicians knocked on my door and I agreed to use them, I was prepared for another aggravating disappointment. Now, three months later, I'm telling everybody I know to use Lawn Technicians. They've turned lawn care into a profession.

The Expanded Testimonial

In print advertising, you'll usually see short testimonials, two or three sentences long. On TV and radio, they're usually a few seconds, except in thirty-minute-long infomercials, where each testimonial may run for a couple of minutes. In online media, there is a prevailing, popular (and entirely incorrect) belief that everything must be brief. Even though short is the norm, there may be cases where you'll want to use an expanded testimonial. As a matter of fact, the long, story-style testimonial can be the basis for an entire full-page ad or newspaper insert, an entire direct-mail piece, or an entire website.

Following is one of my longest tenured "students" and long-time Glazer-Kennedy Insider's Circle™ Member Dr. Gregg Nielsen's patient and public newsletter articles that is, in essence, an expanded testimonial. Every month he does one of these, ranging from a third to a half to a full page, featuring the story of another particularly interesting or made interesting patient like Motocross Mike. I recall seeing a rodeo clown, a downhill ski racer, a local firefighter, a ballerina, and a chef featured. In regular publishing, these are called human interest stories, a staple of one of the most popular magazines of all time, *Reader's Digest*. Dr. Nielsen is a phenomenal marketer. He and his staff and his patients have a lot of fun with his advertising. He's well worth following, which you can do at *www.DocNielsen.com*.

Waterford Chiropractic Office * Monthly Patient Newsletter
* Our 25th Anniversary (Nov-Dec 2010) "End Of The Year" Issue *

Dr. G.E. Nielsen, D.C.
505 Aber Drive
P.O. Box 86
Waterford, WI 53185-0086

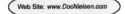
Web Site: www.DocNielsen.com

Phone: (262) 534-3767
Fax: (262) 534-2363
Toll Free: (800) 359-3765
email: docnielsen@aol.com

"Motocross Mike" Lands Hard In Dr. Nielsen's Office!

Dear Friends:

Welcome back to another exciting issue of our multi-award-winning monthly patient newsletter that's published every other month. In this exciting issue we'll jump to Dr. Nielsen's newest wacky patient: "Motocross Mike".

What The Heck Is Motocross?

Motocross is a French word, combing "motorcycle" with "cross country". The sport of motocross was popularized in Europe during the 50's & 60's, primarily in Western Europe. Most events were held in open fields and pastures, and the best riders were from Europe. Even today, motocross is run outdoors, on natural terrain tracks. The races are longer (typically close to 40 minutes) and the tracks have higher top speeds.

Who The Heck Is "Motocross Mike"?

Motocross Mike is just a regular guy who works all week to get enough money to go completely nuts on the weekends and race motorcycles through farm fields.

Mr. Mike crawled into Dr. Nielsen's office a few weeks ago after "kissing the handlebars" during a rough landing. Experiencing some nasty neck pain and stiffness, Mike found our office and he's been doing great ever since.

Will "Motocross Mike" ever be fixed? Let's just say we do the best we can with what you bring us!

*** UNSOLICITED TESTIMONIAL ***

Dear Dr. Nielsen & Staff:

Thanks a million for being open every Monday. Weekends are brutal for me!

Signed: *Motocross Mike * Waterford*

Dr. Nielsen was hiding in the bush to the left as Motocross Mike flew over the last jump before winning a recent race. As you know, the Waterford area has the best courses for recreational motorcycles! **(Staff Photo)**

When Will The "Flu Season" Strike?

The flu season begins in November and is at its height between the months of December and March. According to the Center for Disease Control (the CDC), one out of every five Americans will get the flu this year. *Are you prepared for the flu season?*

Check this out: Chiropractic care may be your answer to a clean bill of health this season, and chiropractic can give your immune system a boost with a spinal adjustment. Let me give you the facts and a recent study about chiropractic and the flu: A study shown in the *Journal of Vertebral Subluxation Research* in 1997 showed chiropractic care to be effective in treating the flu. Over 2,800 individuals received regular chiropractic care and the result was an average 15% decrease in the incidence of colds and the flu. According to the *World Chiropractic Alliance*, spinal adjustments can help your immune system function better. An adjustment corrects spinal misalignments which can cause problems with the nervous system.

When an adjustment is performed, it releases pressure on the nerves and allows more efficient interaction between your body's nervous system and immune system. When your immune system is healthy it is better prepared to prevent or combat the flu. Regular chiropractic care is beneficial to the body. Preventing the flu is just one of the many positive side effects of regular chiropractic care. *Do you really need a flu shot? Or could great flu-fighting benefits accrue from taking a healthier and more natural approach to fighting the flu? And of course eating right, exercising, and having a healthy body are all important issues in combating the flu as well.* We're here to help...just give Miss Stefi or Miss Marie a call now at (262)-534-3767 for your next appointment. Please call today!

Dr. Nielsen Announces He Is Finally Accepting New Patients Again!

Dr. Nielsen announced today that he is finally accepting referrals again. If you have a family member (or, a close friend) who needs relief from headaches, neck pain, or back pain, they will receive their initial consultation, exam, x-rays (if necessary), and their first gentle chiropractic treatment with a $25 donation to the Waterford Fire and Rescue Squad. Please don't keep Dr. Nielsen's office a secret. Call today for an appointment. *(This is a $50+ value!)* This Offer Expires: 12-30-2010

And Finally ... The Answer To This Month's Burning Question...

Q: *My neighbor told me that chiropractic care can help fight-off the flu. Should I see Dr. Nielsen just in case? Is there any help for me to avoid the flu? And is Dr. Nielsen finally accepting new patients again?*

A: Yes.   --*Dr. Nielsen*

Glazer-Kennedy Insider's Circle™ Member Dr. Gregg Nielsen's newsletter example

Real People Versus Celebrity Testimonials

Real people testimonials are, in my opinion, a mandatory component of a solid marketing message. These typically come from your satisfied customers. When using a number of these testimonials in one message, you want to try to **cover as many claim-benefit bases and as many demographic bases as possible.**

If marketing to a demographically diverse group of consumers, you need testimonials from whites, blacks, Asians, and Hispanics; men, women, married, and single people; and the old, the middle-aged, and the young. On the other hand, if you are *not* marketing to a diverse audience, be certain *all* your testimonials are well-matched with your targeted prospects; any that aren't are a waste.

If you're doing business-to-business marketing, the bases you might want to cover would include small companies, medium-sized companies, and big companies—as well as retailers, wholesalers, manufacturers, and service businesses. Or, if you're aiming at a much more narrow, specific target market, then you must match your testimonial sources to it.

Celebrity testimonials can be effective, but they can also be tricky. If your product or service is used or your business patronized by a known personality, such as an athlete or entertainer, you can capitalize on it. Sometimes even an endorsement of your general industry is useful. Some years back, Joe Montana, then playing for the San Francisco 49ers football team, stated that he relied on chiropractors to keep him healthy. Any chiropractor who failed to make use of this was just plain dumb.

We are a celebrity-obsessed, celebrity-dominated, celebrity-driven culture, and it is foolish to ignore it or insist it doesn't apply to your business; it's smart to capitalize on it.

Over the years, I've helped clients get and use countless celebrities for various marketing purposes—including Florence Henderson, Barbara Eden, Robert Wagner, Art Linkletter, Danny Glover, several soap opera actresses and actors, sports personalities including baseball pitcher Don Drysdale and Dallas Cowboys quarterback Danny White, and the list goes on. My long-time client, Guthy-Renker, was the first to use a celebrity to host a TV infomercial in 1986, and since then their use of big-name celebrities has helped them use TV advertising to build multimillion-dollar brands. As I write this, enormously popular celebrities Katy Perry, Jennifer Love Hewitt, and Justin Bieber are featured in TV commercials for Proactiv. At Glazer-Kennedy Insider's Circle™, we bring celebrity entrepreneurs to our two major international conferences to add sizzle to the marketing of these events and give attendees a value-added in the opportunity to hear from, meet, and get photos taken with these stars. Our roster has included Gene Simmons (KISS), Joan Rivers, Ivanka Trump, George Foreman, and Kathy Ireland.

When marketing on a national scale, you need nationally known celebrities, but when marketing locally, a local personality may prove nearly equal in impact but usually a lot easier and less costly to get. But you should not assume your local business cannot afford a national celebrity. One of our Members got former Chicago Bears player Refrigerator Perry for his *local* mortgage brokerage's advertising—very affordably. Another long-time Member and exceptionally astute marketer, Dr. Barry Lycka, in Edmonton, Canada, used both national and local celebrities for the grand-opening marketing for his Corona Rejuvenation Center and Spa. Dr. Lycka got soap opera stars Susan Seaforth Hayes and Bill Hayes (from *Days of Our Lives*), and from his local market he got Lynda Steele, the anchor of the TV news, to attend the grand opening and participate in its promotion. Well over 500 people attended this event!

The best way to secure a celebrity is through someone you know or someone they know. However, you can go direct or through agents and managers, and one of our Members is expert in this. Jordan McCauley helps business owners navigate the waters of approaching and hiring celebrities as a do-it-yourself project. Get his book *Celebrity Leverage: Insider Secrets to Getting Celebrity Endorsements*, or visit his website at *www.CelebrityLeverage.com*. If you are developing a marketing project significant in size and scope, consulting with me about many of its aspects, including the securing and best use of a celebrity, may be appropriate. If so, feel free to contact me directly, via fax to 602-269-3113.

How to Prove Your Case Without Testimonials

Having made a major case for relying on testimonials to tell your story for you and to prove every part of your case, I must also advise you to not stop there. Also, sometimes you may be strictly limited in your use of testimonials, due to FTC regulations (see sidebar) or other reasons. So how else can you show that your product or service is great?

The FTC and Testimonials

The use of customer and celebrity testimonials is regulated by the Federal Trade Commission, and in 2010, new, toughened restrictions on many uses and users were imposed. Information can be obtained at *www.FTC .gov*. This book, incidentally, talks about best marketing strategies without acting as legal adviser, and neither author or publisher accepts any liability whatsoever for any individual reader's marketing decisions. It is your responsibility to ascertain the legality of your actions.

Association
One of the simplest, easiest things you can do to prove your case is using "by their company, ye shall know them."

The Allen Brothers mail-order catalog (for ultra-high-priced, steakhouse-quality meats delivered to your door) routinely features a list of steakhouses from all over the country who buy from Allen Brothers. This emphasizes the basic Allen Brothers' promise: You can have the same exceptional quality steaks the finest restaurants serve their customers, at home. If you buy and read a lot of books, you know that many authors feature introductions by other famous, often more famous, authors or experts. For many years, in marketing myself as a speaker, I emphasized the long list of celebrities that I frequently appeared on programs with.

BACKSTAGE WITH DAN . . . CELEBRITIES THAT I'VE SHARED THE STAGE WITH:

President George Bush and Barbara Bush
Johnny Cash
Debbie Fields (Mrs. Fields Cookies)
George Foreman
Mark Victor Hansen (*Chicken Soup for the Soul*)
Jimmy Johnson
Tom Landry
Jim McCann (1-800-Flowers)
Lee Milteer
Joe Montana
General Colin Powell
Nido Qubein
President Ronald Reagan
Mary Lou Retton
Joan Rivers
Tony Robbins
Cavett Robert
Jim Rohn
General Norman Schwarzkopf
Gene Simmons (KISS)
Gerry Spence
Joe Sugarman
Brian Tracy
Mike Vance
Zig Ziglar

Pictures

We think the eye doesn't lie, so offering visual evidence of "safety in numbers" can be compelling.

The aforementioned Allen Brothers could, for example, show a map with every city where they have fine-restaurant clients marked with red dots, and every place where they have repeat customers who've been getting home deliveries for five years or longer marked with blue dots. For Glazer-Kennedy Insider's Circle™, we often use photos like the following one of our events' audiences, taken as wide shots, to give a sense of the size of the audiences, while most, if they use such photos at all, take ordinary (nonwide) shots. Everybody knows about before-and-after photos, but most use only static shots (e.g., an overweight woman standing in baggy, "fat" clothes; now-skinny woman in bikini). That second photo would be more interesting and dramatic if she was in a bikini playing volleyball on the beach, or standing in front of a convertible with a hot "Ken-doll" guy in the driver's seat. **IT'S UP TO YOU** to come up with many different, interesting ways to use photographs.

Using photography example—Glazer-Kennedy Insider's Circle™ audience

Math

In raising money for disease research, homeless people, abused animals, and so on, you'll often find statements like "every minute of every day, 14 people die of Disease X. Fourteen every minute." This may be more alarming than saying "every year, 7.3 million people die of Disease X." Seven million is a lot, but there are 300 million or so people in the United States, and a lot more worldwide. Seven million in that context is not that many, and 7 million is a number you can't really wrap your head around. And in today's discourse, billions or trillions are tossed about as comic books and candy money. But fourteen every minute—that sounds like a lot, and it's a more dramatic idea. If you were watching them, stopwatch in hand, someone would be keeling over every 4.2 seconds.

Statistical evidence of "safety in numbers" can be very persuasive.

Same idea, turned around: Every minute of every day, 24-7-365, a new member joins the Whatsis Society! That's about 520,000 new members. And that's a lot. But what if it's every hour—that still sounds impressive, maybe more impressive than 8,760 new members. Obviously, how you present numbers matters. **IT'S UP TO YOU** to identify every stat you've got and to present them in interesting ways that demonstrate something meaningful and reassuring.

Perception

MEDIA

Years back, on many occasions, I was paid as a consultant to visit a chiropractor's office, tour it, check out the office's new-patient procedures, and evaluate what might be done better in order to make patients comfortable, confident, satisfied, and likely to refer. Frankly, an amazing number of times my best advice has had to do with some 75-watt light bulbs and a bottle of Mr. Clean. Which brings us to a discussion of customer perception.

If you visit the dictionary and thesaurus, you'll find that "perception" is defined as the ability to see, hear, and become aware of something . . . form an opinion of something . . . through the five senses. And: a way of understanding or regarding something. And: an impression of something. This means that your customer's understanding of you and your business is affected by input brought in through all five senses, consciously and subconsciously, thoughtfully and intuitively. You cannot define yourself for your customers merely by what you assert—no matter how eloquently, persuasively, or aggressively you assert it.

The reigning expert in designing the most effective customer experiences that create the most favorable customer perceptions is my coauthor of the book *Uncensored Sales Strategies*, Sydney Biddle Barrows. She comes from a very unusual background for a business and marketing advisor. She is knowledgeable, smart, intuitive, and exceptionally perception sensitive. Her approach to Sales Choreography is brilliant. I recommend reading the book as well as visiting her website, *www .SydneyBarrows.com. Free* resources are available there. Here, I will give an abbreviated overview of the concept of deliberately controlling customer perception.

Let's begin inside your business, at its premises. This is relevant to the degree that your customers, vendors, investors, or community members visit your business location. If no one ever visits, there's nominal damage done by a pigsty location. If even one person visits, the damage begins.

Consider types of businesses where what goes on inside the business' premises has changed dramatically. Perhaps you've taken your car to a service station and waited while getting an oil change. The waiting area had old, peeling linoleum covered with grease and two plastic chairs to sit on, a stack of hot-rod magazines, and a coffeemaker surrounded by Styrofoam cups and utensils. Today, chains of "quick lube" centers feature not only speed but usually neat, clean reception rooms with comfortable seating and beverage centers and plasma TVs on the wall. Auto dealerships followed this lead in giving their service departments major makeovers. Some have play areas for children, Internet cafés, business centers, and more.

Or think about dental practices. For a long time they were cold, sterile, functional, often blindingly white. Hospital-ish. Unfriendly, intimidating, anxiety inducing. Today? Many feature elaborate reception areas with gigantic aquariums, entertainment centers, and latte and biscotti bars. In the operatories, you'll now find heated massage chairs, plasma TVs, and stereo headphones. In some offices there might even be spas and massage therapists—friendly, relaxing.

Many businesses have been Disney-fied. Yours probably should be.

If you get a copy of my book *No B.S. Wealth Attraction in the New Economy*, you'll find a chapter about High Point University, where my friend Nido Qubein has worked amazing magic—to such extent that I urge you to visit with notepad and pen in hand if traveling anywhere near High Point, North Carolina. Or next best thing, visit *www.high point.edu*. You'll also find a chapter about Kennedy's All-American Barber Clubs and its reinvention of the barber shop as upscale men's club.

This is creative innovation entirely focused on customer perception. Arguably, all this does not speak to or affect the core deliverables—the academic education at High Point, the haircuts and shaves at the Barber Clubs, the oil change, the auto repair, the dentistry. These leaders in "experience marketing" understand that, as the saying goes, for the customer, perception *is* reality.

Here's a very simple two-question test to apply to your own business premises and everything that is seen, heard, touched, smelled, tasted, or experienced there:

1. *Question #1:* Describe the perception of your business that you want your prospect and your customer to form, have, hold, and convey to others.

It'll be useful to be able to summarize this perception goal in a single sentence. But you should probably start out mulling it over and describing it in much more comprehensive terms.

2. *Question #2:* Does *everything* contribute to projecting that image?

Let me give you a great example of incongruity. For most of my life, I've owned and driven Ford and Lincoln-Mercury vehicles. Currently I have a big, fat, gas-guzzling SUV and I'm proud of it. It was a "lifetime thank-you gift" from a client, Joe Polish of Pirhana Marketing—who was I to refuse? But one time, I had a Cadillac. When I had my Caddy, I had it serviced at the best, most successful, most respected Cadillac dealership in Phoenix. As you might guess, their new-car showroom was immaculate: windows sparkling clean, floor buffed to a high gloss, lighting just so, unobtrusive music playing softly in the background.

Their service department was also smartly run. During morning rush hour, when many people dropped off their cars, neatly dressed young women greeted the customers and offered them coffee. The service technicians were also nicely dressed, with shirts and neckties. The area was kept pretty much free of grease and grime. There was also an air of efficiency that was reassuring. The service technicians each had computer terminals and could pull up your car's service records. From the screen, they knew and didn't have to ask for your name, address, phone number, etc.

So far, so good.

The first incongruity was, I suppose, relatively minor, yet it certainly made a major, lasting impression on my mind: The courtesy cars they used to drop customers off at their offices were Buicks, not Cadillacs. Kind of like being picked up and brought to the spa in a limo and sent home in a cab.

The second incongruity looms larger: The place where you settled your account was sandwiched into a narrow hallway; you stood not in a line, for which there was no room, but rather in an intimate, pushing, annoying cluster of people. You conversed with the clerks through tiny little windows, and the clerk I dealt with on two occasions chewed and popped bubblegum and was devoid of personality.

What's wrong with that picture? A lot. First, it is, in fact, a *picture* that sticks. To be consistent with the perception being conveyed by all other areas of the operation, there should have been a nicely appointed living-room type of area where the customers sat comfortably and the clerks came to them, got the invoices signed, took the credit cards back to the accounting area, processed them there, and brought the finished paperwork back to the customer with a smile and a thank you.

ULTIMATE MARKETING SECRET WEAPON #8: Perception Congruency

Every piece of your marketing "puzzle" should be strategically crafted to reinforce a single, central perception.

I'd suggest, incidentally, that "successful" be part of the image you choose to convey. I find that, in most businesses, customers prefer dealing with successful businesses and businesspeople. I can recall going with a consulting client of mine when he was interviewing and choosing a new attorney for his firm—his company was in considerable difficulty with the Federal Trade Commission at the time, so he was going to be a fat catch for whichever law firm he selected. I thought the conversation with the two lawyers at the first firm went well, but he was skeptical about them when we left. He admitted that he couldn't put his finger on why he was uncomfortable with them; he just was. It was several hours later that the impression maneuvered from his subconscious to his conscious and he was able to enunciate his reason for discomfort: "Nothing," he said, "was going on." The phones weren't ringing, the receptionist was reading a magazine, there were empty work areas, there was no busyness noise. In his mind he translated that, rightly or wrongly—but perception is reality—to the law firm being unsuccessful. And he wanted to place his trust in a very successful firm.

Once I was counseling a chiropractor, brand new in practice, located in a brand-new shopping center at a busy intersection but too new to be fully occupied with tenants. He was suffering from an inordinately high number of no-shows: people who would respond to his advertising, schedule exam appointments, then not show up. His parking lot was nude.

He and his staff parked their own cars behind the center. His practice was so new there were rarely patients' cars parked there. And there were no adjacent tenants creating traffic. "How would you feel," I asked him, "if you started to drive up here for your first appointment?" We parked his car, his staff's cars, and a couple of rented-by-the-week Cadillacs in front of that office; his no-show rate dropped like a rock.

Creating a Marketing-Oriented Store Environment

If you don't have a store, you're welcome to skip this brief section.

Coincidentally and fortunately, I was at a major shopping mall recently and, in a national chain store I won't name here, overheard one well-dressed woman, I'd guess rather affluent, say to her shopping companion, "Let's go—this place is too confusing. I can't find what I want here."

I can't count how many times I've seen a store environment or at least part of a store environment designed for the convenience of the staff—not the customer. The smart store environment quite simply facilitates buying. That should be the primary consideration in every design and display decision: Does it make it easier and more likely that the customer will buy?

Last week, I was in a men's clothing store and was struck by these oddities:

1. The casual slacks, like jeans and twill slacks, were intermingled with the dress slacks.
2. The necktie display was closer to the sport shirts than to the dress shirts.

3. Shoes were displayed only in the window, then all the way at the rear of the store.
4. The walls in the dressing rooms were blank.

What would you do differently?

I think I'd group my sports clothes together in one area and display casual slacks, shirts, jackets, and shoes there. I'd similarly group my dress slacks, dress shirts, ties, jackets, suits, and dress shoes together. I'd put framed photos of my newest fashions and framed testimonial letters up on the walls of the dressing rooms.

Here's my Five-Point Criteria for smart store design:

1. Convey a congruent perception.
2. Present goods in a logical, organized way.
3. Help the customer think with creative idea displays.

I was in a pet store recently, and—lo and behold—in the fish section they had a display featuring everything you'd need to set up your first tropical fish aquarium: the aquarium itself, the underground filter, a bag of gravel, a stand, a light and hood, and so on, each neatly labeled with what it was and what it did. Over by the cute puppies was a similar display titled "The Family's First Dog," and it displayed a bowl, bag of food, box of vitamins, a couple of chew toys, a brush, a collar, a leash, and so on.

4. Educate the customer when appropriate—by display, by continuous-loop video, by live demonstrator.
5. Utilize every possibility—such as wall space—to promote, advertise, and educate.

Some store environment principles apply to nonstore locations, too, even including professional offices. I teach chiropractors, for example, that there are only three reasons for the patient being in the office:

1. to get well
2. to learn how to stay well
3. to get inspired to refer

and that every minute spent there, and everything seen or heard while there, should be related to one, two, or all three of those reasons. That means: out with the magazines, in with interesting, educational literature; out with the background music, in with continuous-loop video; out with the mass-produced paintings of farmhouses and snowcapped mountains, in with charts and posters.

An accountant accidentally heard me talking to a group of chiropractors about this and cornered me after the seminar. "How can I apply that idea to my office?" he wanted to know. I asked him, "What are your clients there for? What services do you offer that most clients need but few use?"

We agreed that his clients were there, first, to get well organized financially; second, to learn how to work in tandem with him to stay that way; and third, to get inspired to refer. We determined that financial planning and estate planning were little-used services. So, out with the magazines, in with interesting educational literature (about financial planning and estate planning); out with the F. W. Woolworth paintings, in with relevant posters and signs. And, without a nickel of external advertising, his practice increased its total services rendered to existing clients by more than 30 percent and doubled its client base through referrals in a year.

I think just about any business can turn its environment into a much more effective marketing-oriented environment with these ideas.

Heat

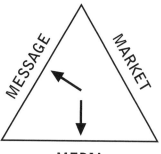

Shortly after moving to Arizona in 1978, I went through a divorce and found myself single and "in the market"—and at that time, the market was Thursday, Friday, and Saturday nights at one place and one place only: an incredibly popular nightclub called Bogart's. Anybody who was anybody frequented Bogart's. All the beautiful people frequented Bogart's. In a city of three-quarters of a million people, there might as well have been only one nightclub. The line to get in the front door was often a hundred people long, but if you knew somebody, you could be granted the great and glorious privilege of buying a $100.00 membership card entitling you to enter via standing in the line at the back door, which was often shorter.

I was there on a Thursday night when it was as I've just described. But that same Saturday, I returned to find a nearly empty Bogart's.

"What happened?" I asked the bartender. "Did they drop the bomb and forget to tell me?"

He shrugged his shoulders and said, "When you're hot you're hot, when you're not you're not."

Bogart's never got hot again. Only a short time later, it ceased to exist. You can sure go from hot to cold in a hurry in that business—and in many others. Best not to get complacent.

ULTIMATE MARKETING SIN #3: Taking Your Customer's Loyalty for Granted

There was a time in America when fads were rare—the hula hoop—but brand loyalty and business loyalty was the norm. A Ford man was a Ford man for life, a Chevy man a Chevy man for life, and in all likelihood their fathers were, respectively, Ford and Chevy men, too. At the local level, your family doctor was your family doctor, for life. The customers of a local restaurant could be counted on for Friday fish fry every Friday. Until we suddenly weren't. We were a Buy American country, too. That has all changed, yet individually a whole lot of business owners act as if it hasn't. A whole lot of business owners *foolishly* expect, even feel entitled to, loyalty from their customers. Sorry, but these days you need to get hot all over again, every new day.

Why do you want heat? To keep current customers interested. To spur them to tell others about you. To attract new customers. To access tens of thousands, hundreds of thousands, or even millions of dollars of free advertising, in forms of publicity, media coverage, viral spread of online media, and person-to-person word of mouth, sometimes called "buzz." You may think the lifeblood of your business is cash, but cash flowing in is actually a result. The lifeblood of business is *interest*. People being interested in it, staying interested in it, thinking about it, talking about it. That's heat.

We can get our clues to heat from fads and from peer pressure, popularity-driven products. Hula hoop then, Silly Bandz recently (but probably extinct by the time you read this). Apple—its iPad. Things you have to have or you're embarrassed by not having them. Even at age thirty-eight, almost everybody's still trying to be one of the cool kids. No, you may not be setting out to create an *actual* fad or fad product, but the things that make a pure fad work can help any business break free of the bounds of boring ordinariness and give it some *heat*.

The Fad Everybody Remembers: An April Fool's Gag and a Sudden Millionaire

The Pet Rock was conceived on April Fool's Day, 1975, in a bar. Gary Dahl was hanging out there with coworkers at a small ad agency when conversation turned to pets—and everybody had stories except him. So he started describing the virtues and drawbacks of his Pet Rock. *Hard to walk on a leash but he can play dead like nobody's business. His name's Rocky but it doesn't matter—he never comes when he's called.* It turned into a comedy routine by committee, with everybody chiming in and having a good time with the fictional pet. In a spurt of odd behavior, Dahl went home and went to work on the goofy idea.

What made the gag work as a product was the Training Manual he wrote that shipped with every rock, basically a parody of a dog training manual. First sales were at a trade show, because he knew if it caught on, distribution would be everything; people had to see it on shelves everywhere they turned. Store buyers snapped it up, and 3,000 were sold at the show. Neiman-Marcus even ordered 500 units. Since he had no capital, he chased free media exposure. *Newsweek* gave Gary and his Pet Rock a half page in November. He did interviews on 1,500 radio shows, there were nearly that many newspaper stories, and by Christmas they shipped the one millionth Pet Rock. Testament to the power of publicity, proof that free advertising can replace and even be more valuable than paid advertising. And Gary had his first million dollars. That was thirty-five years ago, and there's still a lot of people who know about the Pet Rock.

I believe I was the *last* guy in America to buy Nehru jackets. I bought two: a gold silk one with gold buttons, and a green velvet one, which came with white pearl buttons and matching pendant. Honest to God, they went out of style the next day. The fashionistas heard I'd finally gotten on board and that was the end of that. I imagine I could demolish Twitter overnight just by participating. (I don't. I famously refuse to use the Internet at all.) Before my Nehru jackets, of course, there were countless fashion crazes. If you were of my father's era, you might have had peg-leg pants. Of my grandfather's age, spats and a pocket watch.

Kids take to fads even better than adults—although you shouldn't miss the fact that most of those people standing in long lines and even sleeping in tents in line all night to get the latest Apple doohickey are adults. But kids and fads marry more easily and more often. The hula hoop. Tramp tats. Same age group now. Which brings me to something you are undoubtedly already familiar with—Silly Bandz. The forty-seven-year-old guy in Toledo, Ohio, who concocted this thing has wound up selling 24-packs at $4.95 retail to the tune of $100 million and so far birthed a myriad of knockoffs that have racked up another $100 million combined. At one point, he turned down $10 million for his company. He has gone from 20 to 400 U.S. employees plus 3,000 in China, in one year. Peak sales pace has been 1 million packs a week. He has raced to develop spinoff products and do licensing deals with Marvel, Nickelodeon, Disney, Quiznos, you name it. He had his factories and offices under full surveillance so he could look in via his laptop. He did take time off to finish 187th out of 3,000 in the World Series of Poker; otherwise, he has been working nonstop, long hours, seven days a week, sometimes sleeping at the plant, for two years. Industry experts say the only question is when it will stop, and most think it'll stop as if hit in the head with a brick. He thinks he has five years. I'd guess less.

Here's what a lot of you will like: The company has yet to spend a dollar on paid advertising. Sales are entirely viral, kid to kid to kid, and via Facebook, Twitter, and YouTube. The magic ingredient that makes that possible, though, is not the social media so much as it is the trading. There's a trading frenzy. Kids love to trade; I have watched the phenomenon firsthand at Disney with their pin-trading, moneymaking juggernaut. No wonder Disney got this—and projects selling 20 million packs of Silly Bandz by year's end. Being banned at schools will help sales, too. But **the main life force here, that can be moved elsewhere, is *involvement*. Some mechanism for the customer to involve his friends, and those friends to be nearly forced to get involved, so that buying multiplies: 1 gets 10, 10 gets 100, 100 gets 1,000, and 1,000 gets 10,000—fast.** MySpace did it: anybody who took a space had to drag all their friends there or what was the point? You know that pressure; you've gotten it about LinkedIn—*well, that's how I and those in my circle communicate now, so you have to get involved, too, or I guess you won't be hearing from me.* The peer pressure to use social media among kids and adults is enormous, intense, and relentless, just as is the kid pressure to have an arm loaded up with Silly Bandz—otherwise you can't trade, so you're a dorky outcast. Silly Bandz is fueled as all fads are: just by the angst of not being cool. Think iPad. It's fueled like all fads by sell-it-by-zealot, too. But beyond that, Silly Bandz is fueled by this involvement multiplier, a baked-in component that forces multiplication. It's not just about owning them; it's about trading them.

"Forced commerce" is a very interesting idea, by the way. As I said, it occurs at Disney via pin-trading. It occurs differently in in-home party plan selling where everybody attending feels obligated to buy *something*. To a degree, it works with fundraising: people buy things they don't necessarily want from kids raising money for a school, band, team, or a cause. Few are ever able to combine it with the mass, high-speed, viral force that MySpace got, then Twitter got, and that Silly Bandz has.

A client of mine, Darin Spindler, brought all this—including the multiplier effect—together for his business KidsBowlFree.com and put more than 1 million kids and families into their active user database *in a matter of weeks* as a result.

The pertinent question is: What can propel your customers to a frenzy in recruiting everybody they know to follow them to you?

Another lesson of Silly Bandz is the relationship of heat to speed and speed to heat. If you want to get people excited, something exciting has to be happening in a compressed period of time. When such speed occurs, nothing can be permitted to slow it. The owner of Silly Bandz even pays a big fat premium to fly the manufactured bands over from China, cutting delivery to four days from four weeks by boat, so he can keep pumping them out into the marketplace with not even an hour of "sold out" anywhere. He's been working like a banshee. He's in a mad race to go as far as he can as fast as he can, scooping up all he can, with certain knowledge the end is near. Most people never approach their business in this way, ever. They plod as if on an endless marathon with no sense of urgency. They never engineer mad sprints. Well, if you are going to grab peoples' undivided attention and get them all fired up and involved in something, it better be held to a short period of time with enormous intensity. That is transferable to a promotion for any business. You can't make fire rubbing sticks together s-l-o-w-l-y.

ULTIMATE MARKETING SECRET WEAPON #9: Constant Change

We are so interested in the new and different that we express it in vernacular. When we greet someone, we say, "What's *new?*" We *don't* ask, "Hey, what's old? What's the same as it was the last time I ran into you?" Why don't we ask that? Because we just don't care about what's old.

If you want to keep your customers, keep your customers interested, and keep getting your customers to tell others about you, you've got to keep coming up with good answers to the question "What's new?"

During what insiders refer to as "the dark ages" after Walt's death, the Disney empire was crumbling—because there was nothing new going on. Eventually, Michael Eisner came in and recreated the magic of constant, frenetic innovation, and the fortunes of the Disney business machine have never been brighter. In the post-Eisner period, Bob Iger has continued the willingness to invest in constant change.

Words of Wisdom

"I am occupied with 'present' and 'next.'"
—*Norman Lear (age 86), TV/film producer and political activist*

"The only unpardonable sin against Nature is standing still."
—*Robert Collier, famous advertising pioneer, metaphysical philosopher, author of* The Robert Collier Letter Book *and* Secret of the Ages

---

Probably the best example, though, is McDonald's. Hardly a two-week period passes without something new or something different going on at McDonald's: a new product, an incredible offer, a new game, a new free gift. "We can invent," Ray Kroc once said, "faster than the others can copy," and that they do. So should you.

Eight Great Ways to Get Hot And Keep Getting Hot All Over Again

1. Get Prestigious Recognition

Chances are, your local newspaper or entertainment magazine publishes an annual or semiannual "Best of (your city's name)" issue. You have publications with columnists, radio shows with hosts, and TV shows with reporters that all need to be wooed by you—they do have influence in your market! Having well-known people patronize your business and having the media talking about your business makes everybody else want to join the "in crowd."

If you market within an industry niche rather than to the general public, there's less media, but its publishers and editors tend to be more accessible. Some years back, when I was doing a great deal of work with the dental profession, I was able to get myself named as "Marketing Guru of the Year" by an industry trade journal. It wasn't all that difficult. I cultivated a relationship with the publisher over several months.

At least a half dozen of our Glazer-Kennedy Insider's Circle™ Members have managed to maneuver their companies onto the *Inc.* 500 Fastest-Growing Companies list or *Entrepreneur* magazine's lists of top franchisors. I've gotten my books, at different times, onto the *BusinessWeek* magazine and Amazon bestseller lists as well as *Inc. Magazine's* 100 Best Business Books lists.

Any or all of these "honors" can be had for less enterprise than you'd imagine—it's important to investigate the specific criteria of every such opportunity. Such an award has long life but can also be leveraged into publicity in local and national media. It is news.

At Glazer-Kennedy Insider's Circle™, we've created our own annual awards competitions, for Marketer of the Year, Service Business Marketer of the Year, Retailer Marketer of the Year, Professional Practice Marketer of the Year, etc., etc., and many of the winners of these awards do a good job of leveraging the news into publicity in their industry media, local media, and online media. Every Member is eligible to compete.

2. New Products

Voraciously read trade magazines, business magazines, and newspapers—and frequently attend conventions, expos, and trade shows in search of interesting, exciting new products you can offer to your customers. Or create your own from scratch.

Let the fast-food industry be your model. Pay attention to how often Taco Bell, Burger King, Arby's, McDonald's, KFC, etc. run ad campaigns about a specific new product or a limited availability product. McDonald's has "big news" a few times a year when it brings back the McRib sandwich, for a limited time. Yes, *this* works as news!

If you can't figure out how to go this far, at least make your regular products "feel" new. At Glazer-Kennedy Insider's Circle™, for example, we have an annual Members' convention called the Moneymaking/ Marketing SuperConference. It happens in the same month every year and, in structure, is the same every year. It includes speakers, workshops, an exhibit hall, awards, and social functions. It could get stale, but every year we do three important things to make it feel new: one, Bill Glazer and I develop entirely new presentations in keeping with a new and different theme every year; two, we make its marketing thematic; and three, we bring in one, usually two, one-time-only celebrity entrepreneurs as speakers for meet and greets and for Members' photo opportunities. The 2011 SuperConference's theme, as example, different from all prior years' themes, is "Build a Better Business," so construction industry language and images are used throughout the marketing. As something new—this year only—attendees leave with "blueprints" for implementation of strategies from every workshop, the exhibits are in a Hard Hat Zone, and early registrants get a limited edition, souvenir denim "work shirt." There's no reason you couldn't retheme your entire business month to month.

3. New Services

Find new, different, and better ways to be of service to your customers. More and more, people want things done for them. Home Depot went through an evolutionary metamorphosis from being all about do-it-yourself to promoting a wide range of done-for-you services, from carpet installation to kitchen remodeling. A concierge approach is taking hold in many businesses—if we don't do it, we'll get it done for you. The auto repair shop that takes care of my three classic cars as well as my regular automobile not only picks them up and brings them back and provides a loaner when needed, but they take care of required emission checks, get my license plates renewed, provide required photos and information to insurers, and arrange for rental of winter storage space in heated garages. Whatever my need related to things with four wheels, they are my go-to guys. In my book *No B.S. Business Success in the New Economy*, I expound on this as entrepreneurial, miniconglomerate strategy, and as a pathway to synergistic alliances and joint ventures with other noncompeting and complementary business owners.

4. Tie into Trends and News Events

Get involved with what people are thinking and talking about. One of the great direct-response copywriters of all time, Robert Collier, talked about "entering the conversation already taking place in the prospect's mind." This is a powerful strategy, requiring considerable insight and understanding of your market, awareness of what's going on in their lives and in the news, and opportunistic action.

When Bill Gates came under attack by the government for monopolistic, unfair business practices, and every day's news was reporting on that, one of my clients alertly added copy to his ads, sales letters, and faxes talking about how using his product would give your business such an unfair advantage you'd destroy and dominate your competitors just like Bill Gates, but without having to testify or pay huge fines. Response to his advertising went up by nearly 50 percent.

This Vioxx ad was furnished to pharmacies all across America by our long-time Glazer-Kennedy Insider's Circle™ Member Lester Nathan immediately after the prescription drug for arthritis Vioxx was withdrawn from the market. To his credit, he acted fast. The ad was running in newspapers nationwide within thirty-six hours of the drug recall, selling his alternative health product as a substitute. Had he chosen to, he could have used this as a basis for news releases sent and free advertising obtained, putting himself forward to talk about the dangers of drugs and the virtues of natural and homeopathic remedies.

You undoubtedly communicate with your customers and, hopefully, prospects by e-mail and via social media, but to keep regrabbing their interest, the trick is to have "breaking" news. One of the great ad men of all time, David Ogilvy, said that all great advertising has, at its core, news. This is a pathway to breaking news day by day, daily if need be, to keep the heat on.

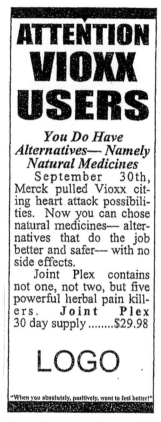

ATTENTION VIOXX USERS

You Do Have Alternatives— Namely Natural Medicines

September 30th, Merck pulled Vioxx citing heart attack possibilities. Now you can chose natural medicines— alternatives that do the job better and safer— with no side effects.

Joint Plex contains not one, not two, but five powerful herbal pain killers. Joint Plex 30 day supply $29.98

LOGO

"When you absolutely, positively, want to feel better!"

Lester Nathan's ad example

5. Tie into Seasons and Holidays

Again, get involved with what people are thinking and talking about. Nothing is more frequently, consistently, and reliably on the minds of more people than the next upcoming holiday. Some of the basic holidays and seasons are listed here, but this is barely scratching the surface. There are thousands of official holidays and special weeks:

Nurses' Week, National Celebration of Squirrels Day, Ice Cream Sundae Week, and on and on and on. Virtually every industry has one or many. Our Glazer-Kennedy Insider's Circle™ Members do such an outstanding job at this, we publish a complete Holiday Promotions Manual featuring their actual marketing campaigns from a diverse variety of businesses. (Visit *www.dankennedy.com/store* for information.)

PROMOTION SCHEDULE

January/Week 1	New Years
January/Week 3	Martin Luther King Jr Day
January/Week 4	Australia Day
February/Week 1	Valentine's Day
February/Week 2	Lincoln's Birthday
February/Week 3	Washington's Birthday
March/Weeks 1–3	St. Patrick's Day
March/Week 3 or 4	Spring officially begins
April/Week 1	April Fool's Day
April/Weeks 2 and 3	Easter
April/Week 4	Italian Liberation Week
May/Weeks 1–3	Mother's Day
May/Week 3	Armed Forces Day
May/Week 5	Memorial Day
June/Week 3	Flag Day
June/Week 4	Summer officially begins
	Father's Day

July/Week 1	Fourth of July
July/Weeks 2–4	Peak of summer—all summer activities
August/Weeks 3, 4, and 5	Back-to-school readiness
September/Week 1	Labor Day
September/Weeks 4 and 5	Rosh Hashanah, Yom Kippur
September/Week 5	Autumn officially begins
October/Week 2	Columbus Day
October/Weeks 3, 4, and 5	Halloween
November/Weeks 1 and 2	Election Day
November/Week 3	Veteran's Day
November/Weeks 1, 2, and 3	Thanksgiving
November/Weeks 3 and 4	Inauguration of holiday shopping season
December/All Weeks	Christmas and Hanukkah
	Winter activities
December/Weeks 3 and 4	New Year's Eve

As you can see, there's hardly a week that goes by that you can't be starting, in the throes of, or winding up a seasonal or holiday-related promotion for your business.

6. Tie into Movies and Entertainment Events

An awful lot of water cooler and coffee klatch conversation has to do with the TV shows of the night before, the movies seen over the weekend, and gossip about celebrities.

For clients of mine, we've tied ad campaigns, marketing, and publicity efforts to a wide variety of TV and movie properties, from *Desperate*

Housewives to the latest James Bond movie. NAPMA, the National Association of Professional Martial Artists, coordinates brilliant promotional campaigns for its member academies and schools with virtually every kid- and family-oriented martial arts movie that gets to theaters. *Kung Fu Panda* provided an enormous opportunity, and as I'm writing this, they are gearing up for the sequel to *Kung Fu Panda*. They will have ads, mailings, online content, games and contests, and group movie nights, and the local school owners will be encouraged to use the movie as a reason for contacting their local media and offering themselves to be interviewed about how martial arts builds character and self-esteem as well as physical fitness in kids.

There are, of course, copyright and trademark issues to be cautious about when tying to such things as TV shows and movies, and this book is not a source of legal advice. You are solely responsible for the legality of your business activity.

7. Piggyback on Others' Fads, Even If Unrelated

I don't know about you, but if someone had come to me and invited me to invest in a movie about giant turtles who lived in the sewers, ate pizza, sang rock music, and were martial arts experts, I would have whipped my checkbook right out. Sure. Nevertheless, the *Teenage Mutant Ninja Turtles* were big, big, big! And Pizza Hut astutely latched onto their coat-tails, uh, shells. But Pizza Hut didn't own this opportunity. A dentist I know went out and bought some stuffed Teenage Mutant Ninja Turtles, displayed them in his office, and mailed all his patients this offer: bring in any child for a special $9.95 exam and he or she can take home the turtle of his or her choice—while supplies last—free! If I had owned a pet store, a record store, a toy store, or a kids' shoe store—I can guarantee you that I would have run some kind of green promotion the year the turtles got hot.

Fortunately, there's some kind of comparable fad every few months or so. Before the ink is dry on the pages of this book, whatever examples I might mention could be a distant memory, but another opportunity will have presented itself for astute marketers to capitalize on.

8. Write, Publish, or Get Published and Promote a Book

If you can't write a grocery list competently, hire a ghostwriter or use a turn-key, everything-done-for-you service like my friend Adam Witty at Advantage Publishing provides (*www.advantagepublishing.com*). But by some means, put out a book—no matter what your business is. There are many reasons—here are three:

One, it gives you authority, which can aid in creating trust and provide competitive differentiation. In the work that I do with financial advisors, with another consultant, Matt Zagula, and the national sales organization, Advisors Excel, we guide every advisor we coach into authorship of at least one book. Matt's own book, *Invasion of the Money-Snatchers*, provided a basis for evening-with-author seminar events that brought in hundreds of good potential clients. (Note: If you happen to be a financial advisor and would like to see some of the marketing Matt and I are doing in that industry, visit *www .CreatingTrustBook.com*. We are also coauthors of a book for financial advisors, *Creating Trust in an Understandably Un-Trusting World*, which is both a how-to book and a positioning tool for us with the industry.)

Two, it is, in many ways, easier to advertise and much easier to get free advertising for your book than for your product, service, or business. As the author of a book about the opportunities in our field, *The Official Get Rich Guide to Information Marketing*, my colleague Robert Skrob, president of the Information Marketing Association (*www.info-marketing.org*), can get just about as many talk radio interviews as he cares to do, can get mentions for the book or reviews of the book in magazines, and can generate a lot of online media coverage for the book. Without the book, trying to get the same access and quantity of media exposure for the association itself would be infinitely more difficult. Suzanne Somers, best known as the air-headed blonde on the old TV comedy *Three's Company*, has, with zero credentials, made herself into an accepted expert on women's health issues and alternative health remedies—by writing books. She is invited on all sorts of major TV shows and networks—from Oprah to CNN to FOX—and is *treated as an authority on these subjects because she's an author.* Being a celebrity helps, yet it would hurt were it not for the books.

Years ago, I solved the problem of slumping ad results and competitive clutter for a Beverly Hills cosmetic surgeon by having him write a book then switch all his advertising from promoting the practice to promoting the book. Recently, at my urging, Clate Mask and Scott Martineau, clients of mine and the top guys at a marketing software company, InfusionSoft, wrote a terrific book, *Conquer the Chaos: How to Grow a Successful Small Business Without Going Crazy*, and did such a great job promoting it they drove it onto the big daddy of all bestseller lists, the *New York Times'* list. This is a business-to-business company, not a consumer products or services business. With no disrespect intended, its authors are *self-appointed* experts. (I'm a huge believer in self-appointment.) Theirs is still a small albeit fast-growing company; they are not yet famous CEOs. If they can put together a good, valuable book and promote it so successfully, who says you can't? And be assured: They have many doors open to them as authors that would be closed if they wanted to get free advertising for their software company. Authorship gives you unique status.

Get Publicity and Motivate Customers by Doing Good

Business tie-ins with charities occur all around you, all the time. But you don't need to be a big company or deal with a major national charity to get in this game, and for the local small business, working with a local charity can be a better opportunity, better appreciated by the community and your customers, and better embraced by local media.

Dr. Gregg Nielsen, a small-town chiropractor discussed earlier in this book, consistently does a good job with promotions for his practice that benefit his community and garner favorable media coverage. Following are two simple sales letters Dr. Nielsen used in the months of October and November, mailed to past "lost" patients, patients, and others who had expressed interest in his services. Each letter includes a brief mention of a donation to the community's fire department. Also shown is the photograph and caption that appeared in the local newspaper—free advertising! This promotion brought 110 patients in the door from a very small mailing and the media attention.

Another great example comes from Bill Glazer, who linked his stores' fiftieth anniversary promotions to Habitat for Humanity via a unique celebrity-autographed tie auction. This used both a celebrity and charity tie-in.

Dr. Barry Lycka, a business and marketing consultant to cosmetic surgeons, frequently relies on publicity to promote his own practice. He received coverage in over 100 newspapers nationwide when he initiated a program providing free cosmetic surgery to victims of domestic abuse.

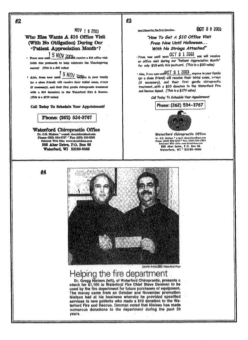

Dr. Gregg Nielsen's October and November sales letter examples

Bill Glazer's celebrity tie auction example

The Basic Tools for Getting Free Advertising: The Press Kit and the News Release

A press kit is a folder or booklet of basic information about you, your business, product, or service; your qualifications as an expert; and your background that can be universally used with any media contact as well as bankers, lenders, investors, vendors, even clients or customers. You will also want its online brother in place: a website or section of your website *specifically for the media* that delivers the same basic items as a traditional offline press kit. The online version offers advantages, of course: you can appear in video and talk to the media; you can have samples of your best, prior interviews there to hear or view; and you can drive media contacts to it by clicking on a link. Both offline and online versions need to include these required items:

1. A biographical sketch and/or resume.
2. A chronological history of your industry and your business, product, or service.
3. Photos of the business, product, or service.
4. Photos of you in action with your product or service, you with famous people, you being interviewed on TV or other media.
5. Copies of any articles or excerpts from books you've written.
6. Copies of articles about you and your business, product, or service.
7. Position statements or press releases—such as those about studies, surveys, polls, new products, nonprofit affiliations, awards received, etc.
8. A list of subjects on which you can be called to comment as a qualified expert.

In addition to the basics, you need some "wow factor" additions, and you need to make the basic items interesting and persuasive, yet still easy for a busy, impatient talk show booker, producer or host, journalist, or other media person to use.

Your press kit can be sent with a cover letter to every radio station producer or manager, every TV station producer or manager, every newspaper editor, every magazine editor, individual show hosts and producers, and individual columnists. Your cover letter may suggest a particular reason to schedule you as a guest now or, more generally, suggest that your press kit be kept on file and that you be called on when they need an expert from your field. Then, periodically, you can mail and e-mail new information to this same list of targets.

This is usually your first contact with a list you've compiled of media targets who might be interested in you and who could be useful to you. If you become known to these contacts as an interesting, knowledgeable source of information, you will get opportunities.

The other basic tool is a good press release. You can create one press release after another, linking yourself or your business to timely events. Best of all, press releases can be sent via broadcast fax and e-mail to radio stations and other media at nominal cost.

The media is increasingly looking to YouTube and social media such as Facebook and LinkedIn for sources and news and human interest stories, so you want presence and activity there if in pursuit of publicity.

A renowned expert in using press releases successfully is my speaking colleague, Dr. Paul Hartunian. Paul is the man who actually did sell the Brooklyn Bridge—well, little hunks of it anyway, to the tune of hundreds of thousands of dollars, all via free advertising, i.e. radio interviews, all created by press releases. For that and other products and businesses, he has been on *The Tonight Show, Oprah, Sally Jesse Raphael,* on CNN, even profiled in *Forbes* magazine. He has generated millions of dollars of free yet valuable advertising via simple press releases. One of the biggest points Paul hammers home is that the media is *not* interested in giving you free advertising, but the media *is* eager for information and stories that will intrigue, interest, or entertain their readers, listeners, and viewers.

You can find publicity resources by Paul at *www.hartunian.com.*

I have a little personal experience with Paul's point. I got my three *NO B.S.* books featured on the prime-time evening news on one of the three networks in Cleveland, one of my home cities, but the station had no interest whatsoever in giving my books free advertising or directly promoting business books. They were intrigued by the "oddity" of a local resident who raced harness horses, actually drove in the races, and wrote business books. So I was interviewed by the sports reporter, not the business reporter. I was in my racing colors, standing next to a horse. But the books were nicely displayed on bales of straw and shown in the segment, which aired twice. Mission accomplished.

This circuitous path to publicity is something I've personally used often. For the past year or so, I've been writing a weekly political opinion column published online by BusinessAndMedia.org, affiliated with the prestigious Media Research Center in Washington, D.C. Every so often one of these columns really hits a nerve, and I get a flurry of invitations to appear as a guest on radio talk shows to be interviewed about that particular column. When I do, I promote BusinessAndMedia.org, but I also work in mention of my business books, Glazer-Kennedy Insider's Circle™ and its websites, and often even direct offer of membership. The listeners to conservative political talk radio include a great many small-business owners, entrepreneurs, and sales professionals, so my "message to market" match is perfect. But I would find it difficult and arduous to secure these free advertising opportunities with this media if I were trying to get on these shows to promote books or a business rather than being invited on as a columnist. However, direct advertising of yourself for any purpose to all radio and TV show producers and hosts is viable and is best accomplished via a service called Radio/TV Interview Report and a form of speed dating with media, the National Publicity Summit, both provided by my clients Bill and Stephen Harrison, publicity mavens extraordinaire! You can investigate their services at *www.FreePublicity.com* and *www.MillionDollarAuthorClub.com*.

Your Only Choice

One of two things is happening with every business, minute by minute, hour by hour, daily, weekly, monthly—either the business is hot, generating lots of heat and getting hot, or it is quickly cooling off and in danger of going cold.

Action

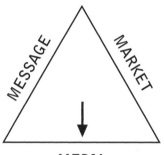

My friend Robert Ringer, best known as the author of the legendary bestselling book *Winning Through Intimidation,* wrote another book that need not have its covers opened for you to get the thrust of its message. It is titled: *Action: Nothing Happens Until Something Moves.* In my book, *No B.S. Wealth Attraction in the New Economy,* one of my Wealth Magnets presented is simply Do Something.

Far too many business owners sit and wait. If they invest in advertising and marketing, they may feel that is enough, and such investment entitles them to success. Others are resource strapped and may feel they are handicapped and unable to effectively promote their businesses. Both are wrong. My motto is: There is always something that can be done—now. And regardless of how much or how little monetary investment is being made in marketing, there are things that can be done personally or by direct delegation, using manual labor and "shoe leather" in place of money, improving process.

Getting Customers Without Going Broke

Early in my business career, I was wisely advised, "Boy, the first thing you got to do is avoid going broke while you're getting rich and famous." Had I paid closer attention, I might very well have saved myself from considerable financial strife. Observing others, I've noticed how frequently entrepreneurs bankrupt themselves with expensive advertising and marketing schemes when their interests would be better served by low-cost methods. When you stop to think about it, it's easy to buy customers—given enough money (or credit), any idiot can build up a business, and many idiots have, using up millions of dollars of stockholders' equity in the process. The genius is in getting customers and making sales without having to use up a huge chunk of capital to do it. The ideas in this chapter are dedicated to that objective.

It's Opportunity Calling!

The phone rang persistently in the little shoe store where I was buying a pair of shoes. Finally, after six rings, the clerk at the counter said, "Dammit—I'm busy," but grudgingly answered the phone. Guess how he sounded to the caller?

This attitudinal error must occur a million times a day in every imaginable type of business, as the incoming call "interrupts" the important work. Fix this and you've taken a giant step forward in attracting new customers as well as retaining the ones you have.

An inbound call can be many things: the tax collector, your mother-in-law announcing a surprise two-week visit, or the merchant next door reporting that your roof is on fire. These calls have varying degrees of importance. But the call can be and often is from a prospective customer, present customer, or past customer, and that is Opportunity calling! These calls must not be thought of as interruptions.

If the call is from a prospective customer, the job of the person handling the call must be clearly defined, understood, and enthusiastically pursued: to get the customer into the store or to get her name, address, and phone number, or to set up an appointment. It is not just to dispense information. This inbound call is a *sales* event, and it must be put in the hands of a person who is or is trained to be a salesperson, with a positive attitude about being in this role. A great resource for small-business owners who need to get their folks answering their phones doing a much better job, and then mystery-shopping them on an ongoing basis, is Chris Mullins, an expert coach in this area. Visit her website at *www.mullinsmediagroup.com.*

These same inbound calls are also opportunities to capture good leads for subsequent follow-up. Let me tell you one of the most instructive true marketing stories I have ever encountered:

The owner of a large auto-parts store was extraordinarily frustrated with his advertising, complaining about weekly expenditures of tens of thousands of dollars in the newspaper, on radio, and on television, all yielding few customers. But a conversation with his employees revealed their frustration with the constant ringing of the phone—calls from people asking questions, constantly interrupting them. A Saturday in his store provided a count of over 200 incoming calls. Here's how everyone was handled, with varying levels of courtesy and friendliness:

"XYZ Auto Parts—how can we help you?" The caller would then state his business. Most often, his inquiry sounded like this: "I saw (heard) your ad—how much is a flibittygibbet for a '68 Ford?"

The answer then went like this: "Lemme look it up—hold on . . . still there? It's sixty-two fifty." Click.

As you can immediately detect, there was no problem at all with this guy's advertising. And, to be fair, his people really weren't at fault, either. *He* was the problem. *He* was the one who had no earthly idea what was going on inside his own business. *He* was the one who had failed to educate his people about the importance of these calls. *He* was the one who had failed to train his people in effective handling of the calls. *He* was the one who had failed to motivate his people. *He* was the one who had failed to monitor their performance.

Here's what we did:

1. We devised a new phone script to capture the caller's name, address, and number. This made every call valuable, even if it was not immediately converted to a sale or a customer rushing down to the store. Without this, many calls had zero value. More value with no more cost!
2. We taught the script to all the employees who took calls.
3. We instituted a reward pool of fifty cents per captured name, address, and phone number, divided at day's end by everybody working that day.
4. We added a "telephone up-sell" to the script: an immediate offer of a $100.00-value coupon book with discount coupons for a variety of auto care products sold at the store plus a free car wash coupon from a local car wash—for $19.95.

> **ULTIMATE MARKETING SECRET WEAPON #10:**
> **Capture Callers' Identity and Market to Them**

Immediately, with this strategy, the number of callers converted, ones who came into the store that same day, increased significantly. But much more importantly, a lot of callers who did not quickly come to the store did provide their contact information. With a series of follow-up mailings over six weeks, the store captured more than 50 percent of the callers as customers! Further, one employee who refused to get with the program was exposed as a toxic influence and fired. The other employees had an opportunity to pocket some extra spending cash just for collecting information, which improved their morale.

Make Sure Your Employees Are Helping Your Cause

The entire issue of employees getting with your program or refusing to get with it and what to do about it, and broader, how to make your team perform profitably, is addressed in detail in my book, *No B.S. Ruthless Management of People and Profits*. The sabotage of advertising and marketing by poorly performing, poorly managed staff is more common than dirt on the ground. This book, *No B.S. Ruthless Management*, is a vitally important companion to any Ultimate Marketing Plan. Get it from any online bookseller or bookstore or, for information, visit *www.NoBSBooks.com*.

ULTIMATE MARKETING SECRET WEAPON #11: The Telephone Up-Sell

In addition, we added revenue and profit with the telephone up-sell. I suppose $19.95 may not sound like much, but this store was getting 200 calls during a weekend. Soon, about twenty of these callers were buying the $19.95 coupon book: $399.00 × 52 Saturdays = $20,748.00 per year. More importantly, 20 people × 52 = 1,040 new customers just about *guaranteed* to come into the store because they've paid for the privilege of buying things there!

You're familiar with the phone up-sell if you've ever ordered by phone from a well-run catalog company. After the operator has taken your order, she'll usually do a Columbo: *Oh, just one more thing . . . we have a special offer just for today's callers—may I tell you about it?*

This is a great illustration of a broader marketing principle, not restricted to making the inbound calls more valuable: digging into the little intricacies of your business, into every interaction with prospects or customers, into every activity, to find opportunities to squeeze out more income juice. If you want to increase income without increasing financial investments in advertising or marketing, this is the path.

Reach Out and Grab a Customer

Fact: the telephone lines run in both directions, in and out. According to Bernie Goldberg, author of the book *How to Manage and Execute Telephone Selling*, someone making outbound telemarketing calls to homes can average twenty-five to thirty-five dialings per hour and ten to fifteen completed calls per hour; someone calling businesses can make twenty to thirty dialings and five to ten completed calls per hour. If a person costs you $5.00 per hour and completes just five calls, that's a cost of $1.00 per presentation; if the person gets ten done, you're down to a cost of fifty cents per presentation. This is comparable to or less than other advertising and marketing methods and much faster to get done.

Why the telephone? Well, just about everybody's got one. And just about everybody answers it when it rings. They may skip your ad in the newspaper. They may throw out your mail or leave your e-mail unopened. But when the phone rings, they answer.

Sadly, "cold" telephone prospecting to consumers is now outlawed for all who've put themselves on the Do Not Call Registry, dicey with others, and less welcome by many than ever before. However, telephone follow-up to people who have expressed interest in your business and given you permission to follow up with them is still viable, and telephone conversation with interested prospects remains one of the most direct, cost-effective marketing tools available to us. Also, Do-Not-Call laws do not affect true B-to-B situations, so telephone prospecting to business owners is still open frontier.

For a printing company, I had a list compiled of small businesses and phone numbers from the area immediately surrounding the shop, created a simple phone script, and made a competition out of it for the five employees, none of whom were salespeople or telemarketers. They each found the time to make one call per hour, eight calls a day. The one who got the most new customers during the week got $100.00. The shop made forty calls a day, 200 calls a week, for $100.00—fifty cents each. The shop also gained an average of ten new customers each week. ANY business could copy this idea.

Quite a few years ago, Fran Tarkenton, former NFL superstar turned businessman, with whom I had the pleasure of coauthoring *The Be Your Own Boss System* for *Entrepreneur* magazine and with whom I've worked on two TV infomercials, got the idea of selling advertising space on airline ticket jackets. He struck a deal with an airline, then faced a question: How best to get the advertisers under contract? Fran chose the simplest, cheapest, fastest way he could think of. He locked himself in a New York City hotel room for several days and called prospects on the phone. The strength of his name was enough to get through to decision-makers; other marketers have to find other ways to get that done. In less than a week, Fran sold millions of dollars of advertising contracts for his newly invented medium to major national corporations and made himself a lot of money.

There is one overwhelmingly superior way most businesses should use telemarketing, if they use it only one way:

ULTIMATE MARKETING SECRET WEAPON #12:
Telemarketing after Direct Mail

Almost without exception, a telemarketing campaign linked to direct mail increases the initial direct-mail results by 500 percent to

1,000 percent! And, this is even truer when marketing to present or past customers with whom you have a relationship. Most business owners do not do this, but they could and should. If mailing to established customers about, say, a sale or special event, having someone call each one several days after the mailing and several days before the event, to make sure they received the announcement, extend a personal invitation, and tell them about a gift or promotion not mentioned in the printed literature, can dramatically boost overall response.

In cold prospecting, B to B, the script can be as simple as this proven template:

1. Identify Yourself
   This is John Smith from ABC Widgets calling.

2. Reason for Calling
   I'm calling to arrange for delivery of a useful free gift, <identify gift>, for the person in your company responsible for purchasing widgets.

   OR

   I'm calling to follow up on my letter to the person in charge of purchasing widgets, to arrange for delivery of his free gift.

3. Identify Decision-Maker
   Who in your company handles widget purchasing?

4. Get to the Decision-Maker
   May I speak to Mr. Widget Buyer for just three minutes, please?

5. Get Past Screening
   Rather than leaving my name and number, I'd very much appreciate setting a time that I should call back—I need to arrange for delivery of

his gift with him personally within two days. (ALTERNATIVE CLOSE) Would it be better if I called back at (insert time) or (insert time)?

6. Repeat 1 and 2 with Decision-Maker

Mr. Widget Buyer, I'm John Smith from ABC Widgets. As part of our (insert month) new-customer promotion, your company has been selected to receive, as a free gift, (inset whatever the gift is) just for (insert desired result: coming in to store this week, setting up an appointment, whatever), and I'm calling to arrange for you to receive this gift.

7. Ask for the Desired Action

I'd like to personally bring your gift in and give you a brief demonstration of the ABC Widget in action. Would tomorrow morning or afternoon be better for you?

OR

I'd like to set your gift aside with your name on it, but I have to know when you'll be coming in. Will tomorrow morning or afternoon be better for you?

YCDBSOYA

My father had a pair of cufflinks when I was a kid that were black squares with raised gold letters: YCDBSOYA. The letters stand for:

You Can't Do Business Sitting On Your Ass

I own the cufflinks and wear them often. I believe in the principle and have lived it for thirty-plus years. Hustle. Even big business leaders hustle. Pay attention to Donald Trump, who I've appeared on programs with as a speaker. He hustles every single day. When I have a book to promote, I hustle: I do radio interviews, teleseminars, book signings and seminar tours (four cities in four days once), news releases, send out promotional copies to centers of influence, make personal calls to ask others to publicize my book, and more. Usually, I invest money in advertising and promotion. But I also invest hustle. You have a business to promote, not a book. But each month you could think of your business as a new book coming out, with you as its author, in a desperate and urgent race to make sure it doesn't die on arrival and sells a respectable enough number of copies to stay on bookstore shelves for months to come.

A few years ago, a favorite restaurant of mine failed during its summer slump. But at no time did its owners get up off their butts and go out into the community door to door to hand out coupons or flyers. Or go to the phone and make telemarketing calls. Or do anything else that was proactive. They didn't hustle. They just sat there and died.

In the same community, that same summer, a young chiropractor got ready to open his new practice—with at least a dozen competing chiropractors surrounding his office already established in the area. He spent one full month prior to opening going door to door, house to house, introducing himself, asking the residents about the area and their health interests, and making friends. He knocked on more than 2,000 doors that month. And from the first day he started seeing patients, his practice has prospered. Its first year it outperformed all the established practices in the area.

There are three types of people: those who make things happen, those who watch things happen, and those who wonder what happened. I think you'll find that most successful businesspeople you know are in the first category.

Take-One Boxes and Contest-Entry Boxes

Everything from cosmetic makeovers and spa memberships to vacation clubs and credit cards are successfully promoted via take-one boxes and contest-entry boxes placed in businesses.

The purpose of these box systems is, of course, to collect names of somewhat qualified prospects for follow-up by mail or phone. A box can cost as little as a couple of dollars and, located in a busy business, collect hundreds of leads each week. A retail business that I had an interest in for several years had its managers drop off contest-entry boxes at outdoor bank ATM machines on Friday evenings and pick them up Sunday evenings to collect hundreds and hundreds of leads for follow-up. The banks probably would not have approved of this gambit, but I will tell you, it was very effective.

For several years, I consulted with a company marketing home security and fire protection systems by bringing homeowners to group presentations at local restaurants, as winners of free dinners. They got all their leads from contest-entry boxes placed (with permission, unlike the previously mentioned guerrilla use of ATM locations) in gas stations, convenience stores, other retail stores, beauty salons, etc., all over each town where they had sales reps.

If I had a business that could effectively follow up on leads by mail or phone, I would develop a contest-entry box and hire a reliable, ambitious college student or, probably better, a retired person in need of extra income to place a number of the boxes and then service them weekly or biweekly, and then pay the person a bonus based on the number of leads or the number of leads converted to appointments or customers.

When using a contest-entry box system, it's important to offer and honestly deliver a valuable, appealing first prize. In Phoenix, weekend getaways to cooler San Diego work very well. But, although not announced in advance, every entrant wins a second prize.

Let's say you want to promote an Italian restaurant and you want to specifically increase your weekday early dinner traffic. First, you get ten contest-entry boxes placed in nonrestaurant businesses, probably in a circle around your restaurant. Second, you collect all the leads every week. Third, you or somebody else calls these leads or you send mail to these leads with this message:

> Thank you for entering our San Diego vacation contest. Unfortunately, you did not win the first prize—it was won by Mr. and Mrs. Jones of Glendale, Arizona. However, you have won a valuable second prize: the enclosed certificate entitles you and your spouse or friend to a 2-for-1 dinner deal at our beautiful Italian Ristorante on 12th Street, Monday through Thursday from 5:00 P.M. to 7:30 P.M. With this certificate, you pay for just one dinner and get a second dinner of equal or lesser value free! Enclosed is a miniature copy of our menu so you can see in advance the tremendous variety and reasonable prices we offer.
>
> Please call for reservations and redeem your certificate within the next twenty-one days.

If a strategy like this seems primitive to you, you're right; it is. But that doesn't negate its stubborn effectiveness. Even as the Internet surrounds us, technological advances abound, and media choices proliferate, you will still find flyers stuck up on community bulletin boards in coffee shops and you will still find take-one boxes all over the place if you open your eyes to them. That's because they still work.

If a strategy like this seems labor-intensive and inefficient to you, you are right about that, too. But shoe-leather and manual labor are substitutes for spending money.

The Power of Cooperation

Cooperation can be carried too far (a camel being a horse built by committee), and I am not a big fan of groups. But I do believe in strategic alliances.

ULTIMATE MARKETING SECRET WEAPON #13:
Asset Sharing for Marketing Success

Two noncompeting but somehow related merchants—a pet store owner and a veterinarian, a restaurant owner and a theater owner, a sporting goods store owner and a sports-bar proprietor, an auto dealer and a carwash owner—can share their customer bases, their store traffic, even their advertising in order to build each others' businesses and stretch their advertising dollars. Reciprocal customer sharing became more popular in the recent recession. It should be a big part of your Ultimate Marketing Plan all the time. To be simplistic, if two cooperating marketers each create 1,000 customers a year and spend $50.00 each, thus $50,000.00 to do it, and they begin reciprocally sharing those customers, they double their reach at half their previous cost. If you can't increase your income with that kind of math, you just can't be helped!

In this same category of cooperation, there are joint ventures. In the business world there are basically two groups: those with customers and those without customers. Each has a need, although someone in the first group must often be educated by someone in the second. The person with a thriving business and good group of responsive customers needs to be of greater and greater service to those customers, and he needs ways to make more money with his customers without doing more work. He may or may not understand this, but he owns the most valuable asset in the world: customers. Then there's you—the entrepreneur with a product or service or business that would be of interest and value to his customers. In direct marketing terms, he could be a "host" and you could be a beneficial "parasite."

Simple example: The dry cleaner has 500 good, repeat customers. But he's nearly at capacity and couldn't do much more dry-cleaning work without adding equipment and space and personnel. How can he make more money? Well, every one of those 500 customers has carpets in their home, which two or three times a year need a good, reliable carpet cleaner. Mr. Dry Cleaner's not prone to get into a second business. But you, Mr. Carpet Cleaner, can pay him for access, introduction, and endorsement to his customers. That's host/parasite marketing.

A truer joint venture would involve the dry cleaner and the carpet cleaner who partner in opening a new car wash in their town and fuel it by marketing it to both their customer lists.

The absolute all-time master of this in my kind of business, the information products and seminar business, is my friend and sometimes client Ted Thomas, an expert in teaching tax lien, real estate, and foreclosure investing strategies. Ted sells millions of dollars of his books, courses, and seminars every year with no front end. That means he does not invest money in advertising or direct mail or anything else to get a customer of his own, from scratch. Instead, he spends his time finding and forming good working relationships with hosts who already have customers. To give you a quick idea of the power in this, here are the actual net profits from several host/parasite campaigns Ted has engineered, each covering only a four- to six-week period of time: $57,000.00, $15,000.00, $30,000.00, and—gulp!—$210,000.00.

I will summarize Ted's key thoughts about host/parasite marketing:

1. Businesses spend fortunes finding and rounding up customers.
2. You can eliminate your out-of-pocket costs, risks, and experimentation by simply paying a host to be a beneficial parasite, to use the customers that already exist.
3. Host and parasite cooperate to exploit the value in the customers in a way the host couldn't or wouldn't do on his own.
4. Make it easy for the host to say yes. It should involve little or no work for the host, so you need whatever sales letters, materials, website material, in-store signage, etc. that will be used done, tested, proven, and furnished to the host so he does not have to invest time or money creating anything. You need to guarantee customer satisfaction, so the host does not endanger his reputation.

5. Make it an irresistible financial win for the host. And I would emphasize here, do NOT be a cheapskate about this. Consider what it costs you to get a customer on your own!

6. When you have a success, nurture the relationship so you can repeat the same promotion or do other promotions with that same host, and use that host as a testimonial when you approach other possible hosts.

Resources Versus Resourcefulness

Virtually every business owner has at least one time, most a number of times, when, for various reasons, they are cash strapped and feel resourceless. It is possible to be without resources. It is inexcusable to be without resourcefulness. That is about *character*, not cash.

I teach this fact: There is always something you can do. There is ALWAYS something you can do. There is always SOMETHING you can do. There is always something YOU can do. Pick up the phone and make calls. Get on your horse and get out in the field. Knock on doors. Proposition a host. Hustle.

Equity

MEDIA

In my Renegade Millionaire System, one of the differences between rich and unrich business owners I emphasize is that the unrich operate entirely in the realm of income while **the rich think in terms of income and *equity*.** The unrich earn and spend. The rich earn and invest, and create assets.

When you ask a group of businesspeople to list their assets, they quickly write down such items as equipment, furniture, leasehold improvements, and inventory. Many never get around to listing their customers. This lapse is often reflective of trouble in their businesses.

In every exceptionally *successful* business, the customer *is*, is *perceived* as, and is *treated* as the most important asset.

To really get to that point and own that belief, you have to figure out what your customer is or can and should be worth to you. In my book *No B.S. Ruthless Management of People and Profits,* I detail the numbers your accountants don't focus on that you need to, including, importantly, TCV—Total Customer Value. A business' highest and best, and most fragile, equity is in its customers and its relationship with those customers, and preserving and growing that asset value requires and deserves focus and investment. It is a grave mistake to be overly attentive to getting new customers and neglectful of marketing to and nurturing relationship with existent customers.

She Hates His Roving Eye

Men say: *I'm married—I'm not dead!* when noticing women other than their wives. The wives plot their death. I once saw an entire episode of Dr. Phil devoted to women complaining about husbands/boyfriends out at dinner, in a bar, or at a party with them but gawking at or, worse, flirting with other babes. This was also the complaint voiced by a lady after a first arranged date on the even-more-insipid-than-Phil reality show *Millionaire Matchmaker.* It's the last argument I had with my first ex-wife, in a bar, the night before she was leaving, with divorce a done deal. So, how do you think your customers feel when they catch you ardently pursuing new ones while ignoring them? Think they don't notice? Idiot. If they see your ad in the newspaper, in Valpak, hear it on radio, etc. but don't hear directly from you, and they remember you at all, they notice, *and they're miffed.* That's why the headline written by Melissa Ward for a book review in *Target Marketing Magazine* is so good: **RETENTION IS THE NEW ACQUISITION.** Quote: "The traditional marketing funnel is outdated, lopsided, broken, with its gaping mouth acquiring many, sometimes *not qualified* customers but retaining few." She plugged the book *Flip the Funnel*—in which its author says: *"In an acquisition focused world, we pull out all the stops to woo a stranger to sample our wares, yet we ignore the very people who essentially fund our acquisition efforts in the first place. It is tantamount to feeding yourself by holding* *the steak knife the wrong way, by the blade—not only will you go hungry, you'll end up in the emergency room."* (There's more from the book at *www.FlipTheFunnelNow.com.*)

Here's a New Economy factoid for you: Businesses that have managed to make lots of money in the past as churn 'n burners, requiring a monster-sized new-customer acquisition machine, are experiencing severe reversals of fortunes. The fuel eaten by such machines is becoming evermore expensive, too expensive. And don't miss the author's point in this book: *present customers (not new customers) fund acquisition.* The days of profitable or even break-even new-customer acquisition are just about over, for just about every business (and foolish desire for this has, frankly, been stunting growth of many long before this). If you are going to buy customers, you'd better get better at keeping them and *fully* monetizing them.

Here's why businesses lose customers:

- **One percent die.** Not much that we can do about that—if they insist on dying on us, that's sort of unpreventable and irreversible.
- **Three percent move away.** Well, people do move. If they move quite a distance outside our market area, there's not much we can do about that, either, unless, via the Internet, you have a no-boundaries extension of your business. Alan Reed's dairy has over 3,000 customers in his local area but also ships ice cream to people all over the country. Some of the smartest real-estate agents in the Cleveland, Ohio, area (where I have a home) are also licensed in Florida and conduct business in both places because many Clevelanders buy and own second homes in Florida, eventually retire to Florida, and eventually list and sell their Ohio homes.
- **Five percent follow a friend or relative's advice and switch to that friend's preferred merchant.** *You might be tempted to say*

there's nothing much to be done about that, either, but I'd disagree. How come we lost our customer to his buddy's merchant instead of that other merchant losing his customer to us? Best man won, maybe?

- **Nine percent switch due to price or a better product.** Some of this 9 percent can't be prevented, but I'll argue that some could. Why don't we have the best product? Or—if we do—why didn't our customer know that?

- **Fourteen percent switch due to product or service dissatisfaction.** True—you just can't please everybody. So some of this is unavoidable, too. But it's my experience as a consumer that a lot of businesses lose me for this reason, are aware of it, but don't even make an attempt at preventing the loss, just like the clothing store previously mentioned. Incredibly, they give up without a fight.

- **But add all that up and you've accounted for only 32 percent of the losses. Why do the *majority of* customers leave?** Can you guess? Sixty-eight percent switch because of what they perceive and describe as **indifference** from the merchant or someone in the merchant's organization. In other words, they felt unappreciated, unimportant, taken for granted. That's not my theory, remember—that's what actual customers have said.

Neglect and Negligence

Negligence is dictionary-defined as "failing to take proper care." If a customer slips and falls on a loose tile in your store's floor, you are at risk of a successful lawsuit for negligence. That injury could have been prevented had you taken proper care of your premises. Negligence toward the care of customers is not always so clearly visible nor are you likely to be sued for it—at least until you pilot your business to bankruptcy court. But it is just as real. *Neglect*, as a noun rather than verb, is dictionary-defined as "the state of being uncared for." In marketing, perception equals reality; the *customer's* perception equals reality, so a feeling or sense of being uncared for is the same as being uncared for. Neglect. Failing to make absolutely sure your customers feel appreciated and cared for is sin of neglect for which there will be punishment.

How many ways can you commit the sin of neglect? To name a few:

1. The spotlighted advertising of offers to new customers with no direct offer of same or better to present customers, in advance, giving them VIP status and recognition (and giving yourself a good excuse to reach out to them).

2. The website(s) purposed for new-customer acquisition getting constant attention, improvement, monkeying-with, while the website(s) primarily serving existent customers left in disrepair.

3. Putting your top copywriter (self, house, or hired gun) on your acquisition campaigns but having your secretary's assistant whip out the e-mails to present customers in between Starbucks runs, walking the office pet lizard, and picking up your dry cleaning.

4. Obsessing over quantity versus quality, response percentages rather than (comparative) customer value.

5. Disproportionate investment in acquisition versus retention—example: willingness to fund an exhibit at a consumer show at the mall or B2B trade show, but refusal to fund a top-flight customer appreciation event.

6. Insisting on trying to ram what you've got, want to sell, or think your customers want or should want down their throats instead of getting and responding to customers' input.

7. Letting communications with present customers disintegrate to the boring and routine, letting the experience of the repeat or regular customer suffer while investing heavily in creating the best experience for the new customer.

Definition, Please

Notes for those unfamiliar with direct marketing terminology: ACQUI-SITION refers to whatever is done under the umbrella of attracting or obtaining new customers. MARKETING FUNNEL refers to your organized process or system through which leads/prospects are first brought in, converted to buyers, buyers developed to customers, additional products sold, etc. RETENTION broadly refers to the keeping of a customer, typically assessed in simple terms, i.e., number of weeks, months, years, or visits, but more sophisticated marketers factor in the comparative value of those retained, such as transaction sizes and total, accumulated spending, frequency, ascension, and referral productivity. If you are not familiar with the most important math measurements regarding acquisition and retention, refer to Chapters 42 and 43 in my book *No B.S. Ruthless Management of People and Profits*.

ULTIMATE MARKETING SECRET WEAPON #14:
Make the Customer Feel Important,
Appreciated, and Respected

The Attitude of Gratitude

I think the kind of customer service that makes customers feel important, appreciated, and respected begins not as policies and procedures but, instead, as *an attitude* of gratitude. It's easy to get caught up in our work and in our business' problems (and even the most successful business has them) and lose touch with how fortunate we are to even have the opportunity to own our own businesses, exercise control over our own incomes, engage in activity we find interesting and rewarding, and have a clientele capable of and willing to support us. I try to remind myself of this often, and really, really remind myself of it on especially grumpy days. Given my utter absence of academic and professional qualifications, I could just as easily be wearing a paper hat and asking "Would you like fries with that?" as operating a practice as a trusted marketing and business advisor, author, and speaker with a seven-figure yearly income. When I stop at the local convenience store en route to the racetrack where my racehorses are stabled, I see the haggard, weary counterperson and think: "There, but for the grace of arrogance, ambition, initiative, persistence, *and my clientele*, go I."

When someone gives us money for our expertise, professional service, ideas, or products—or in patronage of our place of business, catalog, or website—they choose us from a vast array of other possible choices. When there is responsive audience for my next book or seminar or your Home-Style Meatloaf Week at your restaurant, we are recipients of peoples' interest, dollars, and perhaps loyalty amidst the clutter of intense competition. Most peoples' money is not easily come by. When they give it to us, they may have postponed or gone without something else they also needed or wanted. It's important to think about your customers in these terms, not as numbers, statistics, or accounts. Think *gratefully* about each of your customers and each time they return to patronize you, rather than feel entitled to that patronage or presume it will continue.

I was in a doctor's office one day when he asked his receptionist, "What's our body count today?" And that's not uncommon. I've heard customers called bodies, numbers, marks, even chumps. I've seen owners and managers rage on and on about how miserable their customers are—in front of their staffs! These attitudes have to translate into actions, as all attitudes do.

Although it may sound simplistic, getting maximum total value from your customers begins with valuing them—then translating that attitude of gratitude into action. Finding ways to express simple gratitude individually and en masse and publicly to your customers must be part of your Ultimate Marketing Plan.

The Customer Appreciation Event

Little expressions of gratitude matter, but there's nothing quite like a periodic big event, presented to customers as an act of appreciation and used as an opportunity for customers to naturally introduce family, friends, neighbors, and associates to your business.

To witness one such customer appreciation event done brilliantly, I visited our Glazer-Kennedy Insider's Circle™ Member Alan Reed in Idaho. Here's the story, as it originally appeared in an issue of *The No B.S. Marketing Letter*:

> I am in Idaho Falls, Idaho, at Diamond Member Alan Reed's Dairy, where they have a herd of some 200 cows producing milk—requiring two shifts a day of milking, thousands of gallons; a production plant for their milk, cheese, and, most famously, their ice cream; a store of their own; and a fleet of delivery trucks servicing 2,800 homes (up from only 300 a few years ago) and wholesale accounts, such as local supermarkets. I am here with my video crew for their annual Family Day, when customers and their families and friends are invited to a day of pony and horse and wagon rides, a cow milking contest, roping contest, other games, free cookout, farm and plant tours, fifty-cent ice cream cones, and other in-store discounts, which this year . . . despite the previous night's 75 mile per hour winds, area power outages, and generator breakdowns at the plant . . . **is attended by some *3,000* people. Not a typo. 3,000.**
>
> At the event, names, addresses, and e-mail addresses are captured, some immediate sign-ups for home delivery secured, but mostly, via follow-up marketing to those identified as noncustomers, hundreds of new accounts will be added and hundreds more new store customers created. Inactive customers are reactivated. Heck, the next *generation of* customers is seeded.
>
> Many of the people who come stay on the grounds for several hours; meet up with kids, grandkids, grandparents, and neighbors;

and use the picnic grounds. Some live within miles; some have driven hundreds of miles. There is a county fair atmosphere to it. If you've never lived in a Midwestern or heartland of America small town or rural community, never been to county fairs in these parts, and seen farms only at Farmville.com, this would be a foreign and strange scene to you. To me, perfectly natural.

Regardless of where you live or do business or your type of business, this—the annual (or periodic) customer appreciation event—is transferable, and elements of it are potentially valuable for you, too. The annual big event itself is something I've taught for many years and successfully goaded some business owners into doing well—there was, for example, for years, a Florida chiropractor (now retired) who got attendance at the family-days event held at his lakeside home up to 2,000+ and then needed no advertising or marketing all year long; the year's new patients came from the nonpatient new "friends" brought there by patients, met in person that day, and gently followed up on with his newsletter afterward . . . producing over 300 new patients each year, average value $3,000.00 = $900,000.00. *Done right, and made the kind of event customers bring family and friends to,* just about any local or regional business could create the same once-a-year new customer/prospect collection for themselves. I've seen it done by an insurance agent, a martial arts academy, and a bookstore. Note: You can't do this on the cheap. It can't be blatantly commercial and pitch-fest-like.

An important element that makes this work is "community"— and peoples' desire for it. Of course, places like Idaho Falls have it woven throughout the fabric; people stay put here, multigeneration family businesses and farms are common, kids go away to college but come back to their hometown to live, raise their families and work, and much centers around family, church, and community activities— so something like Alan's event is a natural part and extension of that. It is a reunion and gathering place in much the same way as the community's actual big events—their Frontier Days or Apple Festival or county fair—are. But it is also true that considerable effort is invested in making Reed customers part of a full-fledged, unique community. If your customers do not feel part of a community, you are, in my opinion, failing. And the number who would turn out at your big event is a good reality check on this. Social media can help facilitate this (although Reed's Dairy uses none), but in and of itself it is not enough and certainly not a substitute.

Most businesses remain transactional: They sell things to customers and customers buy things from them, and some of these businesses try to put fences around customers or at least foster loyalty defined as retention or frequency of patronage via quality, service, and mechanical means, like loyalty reward programs or pain of disconnect. Nothing wrong with any of that, but you should understand it falls far, far, far short of people belonging to a community. I grew up in a town where you stopped by the gas station even on days you didn't need gas, just to have a cup of coffee with the guys and whatever other folks were there—buying gas, having cars serviced, or also just stopping by "on their rounds" to say hi. It wasn't just a gas station; it was a place of community. Every drug store and Kresge store had a soda fountain and lunch counter for this same reason; hardware stores had rocking chairs on their porches and chairs inside around a stove in winter, and in small towns still do. (As seen on *Green Acres.*) The Starbucks third-place concept is a throwback. In this manner, these businesses transcend their commodities and transactions to relationships and community. The ability to sustain prosperity in the unprosperous times now with us and in the near future may very well rest on how strong the connection to your community your customers feel.

If you think your business is too giant and global, think again. Go into your numbers. You'll find the 80/20 rule in play, which will shrink your important number considerably. Within that 20 percent from which 80 percent of your sales and/or profits and/or best-by-far

TCV comes from will be 20 percent (20 percent of the 20 percent) making the greatest contribution. Even big businesses are powered by relatively small numbers. They are most likely to respond to community, and, for them, community can be created.

If you'd like to see photos, video, and commentary of my visit to Reed Dairy's Family Day, and see more of Alan's great marketing, visit *www.ReedsDairy.com*. The mail-order ice cream business Alan and I are developing can also be seen on *www.ReedsIceCream.com*.

Reed's Dairy

Reed's Dairy Home Delivery

"I'll tell you why we really like it here at Reed's Dairy. **They do not inject us with artificial hormones like rBST** to make our bodies produce more milk. They know we will do the best we can without those painful shots. The other thing is we are not being pumped full of antibiotics. We just love it at the Reed Farm; in fact we call it the "cow Marriott".
You really need to drink our milk. So let one of our milkmen bring it to you. Sign up today. Call an office human at 522-0123."

2660 West Broadway
Idaho Falls, ID 83402
208-522-0123
www.ReedsDairy.com

"Home delivery beats the hassle of always running out of milk and having to go to the store." Paula Kvarfordt, Long Time Customer
That's exactly what Reed's Home Milk Delivery does is take some of the hassle out of your life. Relax a little and let us bring the milk and dairy products to your door.

Save Time and Money

Think about how much it costs for a "quick" trip to the grocery store just for a gallon of milk. Besides the gas used in your car, how about the other things that just jump into your hand while walking back to the milk cooler? Sugar- laden soda pop, high fat junk food, or those other products you just could do without. Our customers tell us over and over how much money they save with home delivery because they are not enticed to impulse buying in the grocery store. You can also plan ahead since you are only billed at the end of the month.

And what about the time savings. We all have better things to do than stand in the express line waiting to purchase our milk. You will have much more time to do some of those things you have always wanted to do; craft projects, play with the kids, or just take a break. With Reed's home delivery, your milk will be waiting in an insulated door box on your step. There is a way for life to be easier!

"I am writing this letter to thank you for all your years of great service. Moreover, for your outstanding products that are always fresh." D Caldwell

No Bad Hormones in Reed's Milk

Since we are the only dairy in Southeastern Idaho which bottles its own milk, we can totally guarantee our customers there is none of the synthetic hormones in our milk. Reed's milk is the only milk which can make this guarantee.

FDA has tested rbST for many years on cows. They say its safe and there is no difference in the milk. We are not saying they are right or wrong. We have had some food scientists express concern about using rbST. We feel the consumer should be able to make a choice. Reed's milk is absolutely free of rbST!

This means your children will be able to have pure, wholesome milk. Receiving all the nutrition your kids need without the worry of the effects of rbST. With Reed's milk you now have a choice.

Reed's Dairy catalog example, pages 1 and 2

Changing Your Order and Billing

You can change your regular order by emailing us at: orders@reedsdairy.com .We must receive your email **before** 4:00 am the day of your delivery. Put your name, address, day of delivery and your change in your email.

The credit card number you supply us with when you start will be automatically charged every Friday for the delivery you received that week.

Better Nutrition From Fresh Milk

Milk from Reed's Dairy is not hauled hundreds of miles before it reaches your refrigerator. Generally, milk is hauled from the farm miles and miles to the plant where it's bottled. Then it must be hauled hundreds of miles to the store. It's days before you are able to purchase your milk.

Reed's milk is delivered to our customers within hours from the time it comes from the cow. After bottling, our milk is loaded on our trucks and delivered to your door, never being exposed to any light which can destroy precious vitamins. All types of light, florescent or sunlight, can zap the Vitamin A and riboflavin (Vitamin B2) from milk. In fact, dozens of scientific studies over the past 20 years has documented light's harmful impact on vitamins. Your family will benefit from a better glass of milk, delivered to you from Reed's Dairy.

Easy For You To Recycle

Reed's milk is delivered in returnable half gallon bottles. These bottles are a hard plastic bottle which we wash and sterilize before each use. You will not need to worry about the billions of plastic milk bottles which are filling up the landfills. You will not be contributing to this landfill problem by getting your milk in Reed's returnable bottles.

Come Visit Our Dairy Farm

You are always welcome to our dairy farm. You can pet the baby calves and see how they are cared for. Walk out around the milk cows; see where they stay, what they eat and how they are fed. There is a large picture window where you can watch the cows being milked. See our ponies and other surprises we have. Come and picnic in the shade and protection of our wonderful trees that surround our large office lawn. We look forward to seeing you.

Whole Milk	
Disposable Gallon...	4.41
Returnable Half Gallon...	2.18
Two Percent	
Disposable Gallon...	4.30
Returnable Half Gallon...	2.11
One Percent	
Returnable Half Gallon...	2.02
Skim Milk	
Disposable Gallon...	4.14
Returnable Half Gallon...	2.02
Cirus Drink - Gallon...	2.25
Cream-Quart...	4.44
Cream-Pint...	2.83
Fruit Punch- Gallon...	1.84
Reed's Gourmet Choc.Milk-Half Gallon...	3.79
Eggs-Dozen ...Current Market Price	
Half & Half-Pint...	0.87
Buttermilk-Quart...	1.26
Sour Cream-Half Pint...	1.01
Cottage Cheese-16 ounce...	1.93
Cottage Cheese-24 ounce...	2.76
Butter-Pound... market price	
Reed's Cheddar Cheese-Pound...	2.24
Margarine-Pound...	1.19
Bread White or Wheat-24 oz. Loaf...	2.84
Yogurt-Half Pint...	0.60
Fresh Cheese Curds-Pound...	3.57

Reed's Prestigious Ice Cream
Half Gallon... 4.95
Vanilla, Strawberry, Chocolate Moose, Cookies & Cream, Chocolate Almond, Caramel Praline, Chunky Monkey

12 Pack Pop...	6.25
Honey...	
Regular-5 Pound...	13.99
Creamed-40 ounce...	7.86

Geraldine's Bakery Bread
White Bread...	2.73
Wheat Bread...	2.73
Crescent or Parker House Rolls...	3.50
Orange Juice Half Gallon...	4.07
String Cheese 10 pack...	3.57
Reed Farm Potatoes 10 pound bag...	1.57

Reed's Dairy
2660 W. Broadway, Idaho Falls, ID 83402
522-0123   www.ReedsDairy.com

"Thanks for having my milk delivered to your door. Even though you don't have to come to the dairy you should visit me and my other farm animal buddies. There are goats, pigs, sheep and ponies. Oh, yea... those crazy chickens that are running all over the place. I have told the Reed's if I have to be in a corral those chickens should be in a coop!"

Reed's Dairy catalog example, pages 3 and 4

Formal Reward Programs

You are familiar with these. Airlines started frequent flyer reward programs, and banks, retailers, and others followed that model. These days, many consumers' wallets and key chains are filled with cards from the reward programs they're members of. In B2B situations, many business owners try to make virtually every needed purchase through a credit card offering reward points. In some cases, with major corporations and chains, these programs have been so prostituted and commoditized, I don't think they really do much anymore to control choice or provoke loyalty. However, for many small merchants and midsized companies with good relationships with customers, the addition of an attractive rewards program can make a measurable difference in retention and frequency of patronage.

The world-class expert in this is the cofounder and CEO of Royalty Rewards, a long-time client and friend of mine, Rory Fatt. His company not only provides a turnkey, one-stop shop for standardized or customized rewards programs for every kind and size of business, but it integrates it with monthly promotions and marketing programs, all implemented and administered for the business owner. They'll install and run your rewards program for you. For information, visit *www .royaltyrewards.com.*

Make Everyone on Your Team an Ambassador of Customer-Service Diplomacy

To excel in customer service—better, in customer *enthusiasm*—every member of your team has to understand, accept, and live it as a priority.

Surely you've heard that adage: the customer is always right. But you don't have to be in business very long before you know how totally false that is. Although they are thankfully a minority, some customers are grossly unreasonable, virtually impossible to satisfy. Taking "the customer is always right" approach dooms your efforts before they begin. Neither you nor the members of your team will be able to live up to that ideal. I'm not even sure that you should if you could. From time to time, there'll be a customer you will be better off without. I have occasionally "terminated" customers and clients in my businesses, I think for good cause, and always found that the vacuum quickly filled with better business.

A better, more accurate approach comes from customer-service training expert, Frank Cooper, who says, "The customer signs your paycheck." With that in mind, we can design a Customer-Service Diplomacy Program that makes sense but doesn't force us to aspire to the unattainable.

131

Diplomacy is all about being Old World gracious. If you've ever been to a very formal party at a very wealthy person's home, an old country club, or an embassy, you know what I mean. Walt Disney insisted that his customers be thought of, always referred to, and treated as "guests," drawing the analogy that if you treat the customer as you would an honored guest in your home, you'll rarely err. That has remained ingrained in Disney culture long after Walt's death.

I'd suggest incorporating these key ideas into your own clearly defined, written, taught, and managed Customer-Service Diplomacy Program:

1. Greet the Customer as a Welcome, Honored, Important Guest

This means that the customer can never be an interruption. Those who answer your telephones or greet customers when they enter your premises must be professionally educated in good business manners and must use them.

If you've ever walked up to a cash register in a department store and stood waiting while two sales clerks finished their conversation, you've experienced the opposite of this idea—and I'll bet you resented it. I occasionally catch clerks in stores actually talking on their cell phones to some distant party while operating the cash register and bagging my merchandise. I believe it should be legal to shoot them.

2. Be Able to Answer Customers' Questions Knowledgeably

One of the reasons for the early success and growth of the Home Depot chain of hardware, housewares, and do-it-yourself product warehouse stores was the surprising helpfulness and knowledge of their employees. Their idea was to give the kind of customer service found in old, sole-proprietor hardware stores, but in a modern superstore environment with discount prices. Whether or not they are presently true to this early value, I leave you to judge. But it was major factor in their early success.

Anybody in your operation who a customer can get to must be knowledgeable, informed, and articulate, and if you have staff members who cannot be knowledgeable experts about your products and services, then they must have a good means of immediately getting an answer for any customer at any time that the place of business is open.

Some years back, while masquerading as a customer and secretly shopping some residential communities on behalf of a client, I asked one salesman a question like this: "If I give you a deposit today on Property A and then want to change my mind and switch it to Property B before thirty days are up, can I do that?" The salesman honestly didn't know. He should have. But he didn't. And at 4:45 P.M. there was no one he could go to or call to get the answer. So he stalled. Had I been a real customer, this would have been the equivalent of stopping a sale dead in its tracks. (By the way, the correct answer was yes.)

Incidentally, what you think your salespeople or other staff members know and what they know, what answers you assume they're giving customers and the actual answers they're dispensing, are very, very, very often two different things with a shockingly wide gap in between. If you are not monitoring and enforcing knowledge and scripted answers, I promise, what you are getting absent such monitoring is costing you money and undermining your marketing. The axiom is accurate: Don't expect what you don't (constantly) inspect.

3. Prevent Policies from Driving Away Customers

I have given up counting—I no longer know (or care)—how many times I've been told, "That's our policy." In most cases, my response is, "I've got a policy, too. My policy is never to spend another nickel with your business after I've been told about your policy."

Of course, you have to have policies. I run businesses; I know that. But you'd better remember this one: As a prison warden, you can make up all the policies you want to because you've got a captive audience—they can't leave. Your customer, however, has the final option. He can put his money back in his pocket and walk away, never to return. Nothing incenses customers more than being quoted policy.

The very best policy is to create ways to say yes to customers' wants and needs. I've been in restaurants where NO SUBSTITUTIONS is imprinted on the menu in big, bold type; where, if asked, the waitress snaps, "No separate checks." Their policy is "Our way or the highway." An awful lot of basically good customers choose the highway.

Be very careful of permitting logistics or your or staff's convenience to interfere with the most effective marketing, sales activity, or customer diplomacy.

4. Have a Process for Handling Complaints in Place

This is not the place to play it catch-as-catch-can. An angry, irate, unsatisfied customer on the loose in the marketplace can and often will cause you considerable damage—especially in today's Internet age, where anybody can air their displeasure very publicly, to a large audience. At the very least, each one will spread the word to a dozen or more present or potential customers. They will take dollars right out of your bank account. At worst, they may also cause you some grief with the Better Business Bureau, the attorney general's office, or other bureaucracies. Occasionally, a customer driven over the edge strolls in with a shotgun and does some permanent damage.

You need to have a sensible, step-by-step process decided on and in place for diplomatically handling and attempting to resolve complaints. One of my adages is: *Would you rather be right or rich?* Sometimes, who's right and who's wrong is entirely irrelevant. It is potential cost that matters.

Customer Retention as a Profit Center—Lost Customers as New Opportunity

As we've already discussed, a common failing of businesses small and large is focusing all their resources on getting more new customers but investing little or nothing in retaining customers. I try to get business owners to **view retention as a marketing function** *and* **as a profit center.** Dumb companies and business owners view everything spent on established customers as an expense rather than an investment, despite the obvious fact that every discouraged, lost customer bears double the cost: the loss of the customer and whatever value he represents going forward *plus* the expense that must be incurred in replacing him.

> **ULTIMATE MARKETING SIN #4:**
> **Letting a Customer Leave Angry Without First Exhausting Every Means at Your Disposal to Resolve the Dispute**

But, no matter how determined and effective your efforts are at retention, some customers will wander off. Some can be brought back. Generally, it is less costly to tempt back a lost customer than to create a new one from scratch, so, ironically, your lost customers represent a better marketing opportunity than the pursuit of new ones.

The sooner you act to rescue the lost, the better. Set up some kind of system to track every customer's activity, and whenever one goes missing for an inordinate length of time, send that customer a letter and a great offer, coupon, or free gift, or pick up the phone and call to find out why the customer is no longer purchasing from your business.

Don't give up too early or easily. While a quick response to customer inactivity is going to yield best results, lost customers can still be reactivated even after months or years lost in the woods. Include them periodically in marketing for your best promotions, hottest new products, and most interesting events.

The Four Best Ways to Increase Total Customer Value

1. Increase Average Order or Purchase Size

Restaurants do this by effectively merchandising desserts and take-home treats and other products. Industrial marketers do it by expanding product line use and upping the customer to bigger sizes. Catalog companies do it with "today's telephone specials" offered to the caller after her intended order has been taken. At websites, versions of that are the thank-you page with up-sell offer and optional or forced live chat, immediately connecting the website visitor with a human salesperson.

2. Increase Frequency of Repeat Purchase

Using rewards, discounts, frequent buyer clubs, volume rebates, and frequent contact, you can capture a larger share of each customer's expenditures.

3. Offer Existent Customers a Greater Variety of Goods and Services

These people are predisposed to buy from you. In my *No B.S. Business Success in the New Economy* book, I talk at some length about what I call "the mini-conglomerate approach." Given that the most difficult and expensive business function is getting and keeping the customer, it just makes sense to work hard at doing more business with each customer. So, the carpet cleaning company that also offers air duct cleaning; sells premium quality vacuum cleaners and air purifiers; and maybe even owns or is in a strategic alliance with a pool cleaning business, lawn care business, or pest control business leverages each customer to maximum value.

> ## ULTIMATE MARKETING SECRET WEAPON #15:
> ### Developing New Products and Services for Existent Customers Instead of Getting New Customers for Existent Products and Services

4. Get Existent Customers to Bring You Their Friends, Relatives, Neighbors, Business Associates, Employees, and Others as New Customers

Referral activity can and should be strategically managed. Most business owners settle for what they get. We'll expand on this in Success Factor #9.

The Ultimate *Wealth* Plan

Assets = equity, equity = wealth. The quality and value of your assets = amount of your equity = size, scope, and security of your wealth.

Thus, the quality and value of your customers is a bigger and more significant thing to think about than simply making sales. As you translate all the ideas and information in this book into your own Ultimate Marketing Plan, be sure to strategically engineer it to (a) attract high quality, high value customers, and (b) retain, nurture, and grow the value of your customers.

Comedienne-entrepreneur Joan Rivers, who I've had the privilege of once having as a client, writing for, and more recently having her speak at one of our Glazer-Kennedy Insider's Circle™ Marketing & Moneymaking SuperConferences, has a line: "It's no harder to fall in love with a *rich* man." Similarly, it is not much more difficult to bring in ideal, high-value customers than it is to bring in any customer with a pulse, but most marketers think "anybody, everybody, and as many as possible" rather than think about the equity they are creating.

That addresses the importance of selective attraction. Then there is the matter we've been discussing here: retention and preservation or improvement of customer value. The combination of those two determines the wealth your business provides to you and your family.

For more on the subject of wealth, I unhumbly recommend my book, *No B.S. Wealth Attraction in the New Economy*. In that book, I present twenty-eight Wealth Magnets—the strategies, behaviors, and business practices that magnetically attract opportunity, cooperation from others, clientele, and money. One of these magnets is *clarity*. And one of the kinds of clarity that is vital is clarity of purpose, which gets to the question: Why are you here, to develop your own Ultimate Marketing Plan for your business? I urge not selling yourself or the tools given you in this book short with such a limited objective as "selling more stuff" or "increasing income." You can accomplish much more and much more significant goals, but you're unlikely to achieve goals you aren't clear about. Why not apply your Ultimate Marketing Plan for strength and sustainability of your business, for marketplace dominance and prominence, and for wealth?

Customer Multiplication

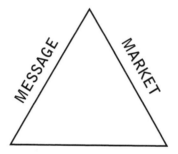

Wouldn't it be nice if science allowed you to just clone your best customers?

Let's begin by recognizing that there is no better new customer than a referral from a happy customer. I don't care what business you're in, this is true. The referred customer has less skepticism and is less price resistant, more receptive, and more easily sold and satisfied.

Most businesses take referrals for granted. Whatever number of referrals they get, they gratefully accept, but they have no proactive plan for stimulating the maximum number of referrals.

How Many Referrals Can You Get?

Joe Girard, repeatedly recognized by the *Guinness Book of World Records* as the world's greatest salesman, has a "Rule of 52," based on his discovery that the average number of attendees at both weddings and funerals is fifty-two. In marketing to consumers, his contention is that each customer has the potential of referring fifty-two other customers. Even if we cut his number in half, ask yourself: Is your business averaging twenty-six referrals per customer? Probably not—most average anywhere from less than one to three. There is room for improvement.

In business-to-business marketing, the numbers are different. I did some admittedly clumsy but I think instructive research: I took executives and business owners in a dozen different industries and had them go through their trade association directories and count the number of people whom they knew (and who knew them) on a first-name basis. The average was thirty-seven—thus each business customer has the ability to refer thirty-seven others to a vendor.

If you would like more referrals, begin by establishing goals and quotas, and holding yourself, your staff, and your customers accountable for achieving your objectives.

The Way to Get Referrals Is with the "Ear" Formula

LISTEN!—and I will tell you how to dramatically improve your referral productivity, with the EAR Formula.

E Stands for EARN

We have to *earn* our referrals. Walt Disney put it this way: "Do what you do so well that people *can't resist* telling others about you."

ULTIMATE MARKETING SECRET WEAPON #16:
Excellence, as Desired by the Customer

If there is one "secret" to maximum referrals, it is that *satisfied* customers do *not* refer abundantly. Enthused, inspired, awed customers refer in great abundance. If customers get only what they expect and deserve, that's not enough. This is not in conflict with what I discuss in other books about finding the customer's GE-SPOT: Good-Enough Spot. Customer enthusiasm comes from being good at what is important to them *and* about finding ways to WOW! them, that they couldn't expect or desire but enjoy or appreciate when it occurs.

Let me tell you about a dentist who multiplied his practice by ten in just one year without even a $1.00 increase in his advertising budget. He caters to children and, after a seminar on creative thinking, he built up a list of 300 things to change in his practice. For example:

■ He redesigned his office to provide maximum comfort to the "short people" who came there. He lowered the reception staff into a pit behind the counter, so they were at eye level with the patients.

■ He hung giant photographs of each dentist and dental assistant along with descriptions of each person's hobbies and interests, so new patients could pick their dentists and D.A.s based on having something in common with them.

■ He gave away free bicycles! Every patient got a "home care follow-through Report Card" for his or her parents to fill out. If the Report Card came back to the dentist with all As, the youngster got a bicycle. (Imagine as little Johnny rides around the neighborhood on his new bike and people ask him who got it for him, he answers, "My dentist.")

- He called each new patient at home the evening after treatment, just to see how the patient was feeling. He called each parent the day after the child's treatment.
- Each new patient left the office the first time with an autographed 8 × 10 glossy of his dentist and dental assistant!

Guess what? At backyard barbecues, PTA meetings, and office lunches, the number one topic of conversation was little Johnny's weird dentist! Pardon the pun, but his practice multiplied itself by ten purely through word-of-mouth advertising.

Most important to understand: his abundant referrals were not inspired by excellence in dentistry. That was just the ante to be in the game. An expected requirement.

A Stands for ASK

I am amazed at the wimpiness of most businesspeople, salespeople, and professionals when it comes to the simple act of asking for referrals. I believe there is a Biblical instruction about this.

Here are the three best ways to ask for referrals:

1. Display and convey your expectations

In doctors' offices, we encourage the use of some kind of display board listing the names of the patients who have referred that month. This list says to everyone who sees it: "Our patients refer—we *expect* you to refer also." It works. And it can be copied by an endless variety of retail businesses. Customers who refer should be recognized in your physical space, in your newsletters, at your websites, and in your marketing so that the idea that "referring is what you do around here" is in your customer's face constantly.

2. Conduct referral promotions

Give your customers cards, coupons, or certificates good for gifts or discounts that they can endorse, like a check, and give to their friends and colleagues. Then give away prizes to those who generate the most referrals within a certain period.

3. Conduct referral events

An insurance agent I know throws himself a birthday party each year and invites all his clients and all the friends they care to bring to the bash. It's usually held in a huge tent, with live entertainment, a buffet, drinks, wandering magicians, belly dancers, and all sorts of other goings-on. Hundreds of clients bring hundreds of other people each year—and the birthday boy gets to meet and make friends with hundreds of prospects.

R Stands for RECOGNIZE and REWARD

A favorite story: A guy rows his little boat out to the middle of the lake for a relaxing day of fishing. Up over the side of the boat comes a huge green snake, with a half-swallowed frog sticking out of its mouth. Feeling for the frog, the guy whacks the snake with the oar; the snake spits out the frog, and the frog's life is saved—and that makes the guy feel good. But the guy also knows he has just deprived the snake of a meal—and that makes him feel bad. Having no food with him, he gives the snake a swig out of his bottle of bourbon, and the snake swims away happy. Two minutes later the snake swims back with two frogs in its mouth.

When we recognize and reward a certain behavior, we inspire more of the same. It's true in parenting, in managing, and in managing customers. When you get a referral from a customer or client, the smartest thing you can do is to make a big, big deal out of it. Call with thanks or send a personal thank-you note or gift.

ULTIMATE MARKETING SECRET WEAPON #17:
Enlist a "Champion"

Elsewhere in this book I told you about the best car salesman I know, Bill Glazner. He has never yet asked me for a referral, but he is so darned good at what he does that, in the span of a few years, I sent him several dozen customers. And he has thanked me for every one of them.

In me, he created a "champion"—a person who champions his cause, who tells everybody about him. A handful of cultivated, appreciated champions can make you rich.

Creating Short-Term Sales Surges

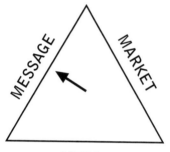

Each business hits its own times of need when a sales surge is important. It's always preferable to sell your way out of a financial problem than to borrow or sell off equity. Often that can be done. There is usually money waiting in customers' pockets. Here are the best ways I know to create a short-term sales surge.

Big Discount, Believable Reason Why

Excess inventory, out-of-date inventory, service time during the off-season . . . such merchandise can often be sold at big discounts, but it's important to remember the current high level of skepticism and cynicism of your public. Many outstanding discount offers fail miserably because the intended buyers "smell a rat."

When you run a fire sale, they'd better be able to see the charred timbers! When you offer an exceptional savings opportunity, there'd better be a good reason. Here are a few "good reasons":

- We're offering this value only to our best customers, as a reward for their support.
- We're extending this offer only to new, first-time customers.
- Frankly, this is our slowest month, and to avoid laying off our great employees we'd rather offer you an exceptional value.
- We've been given a special incentive from the factory and are passing that savings on to you.
- We're eager to show you our new (whatever) and thought that offering this exceptional value would be a good enticement.

One of the best "excuses" for a big sale is Bill Glazer's "Flood" ad. Bill is president of Glazer-Kennedy Insider's Circle™ as well as an advertising and marketing consultant and coach these days. In his former life, he operated very successful menswear stores—a laboratory where he perfected many of the strategies in his bestselling book, *Outrageous Advertising That's Outrageously Successful*. This ad of his is one of my all-time favorites because of its twist on the classic fire sale and because of its use of

Example #1: Newspaper "Advertorial" Promotion

Bill Glazer's "Flood" ad

the entrepreneurial success principle from *Think and Grow Rich* author, Napoleon Hill: in every adversity, the seed of opportunity. I'll reveal two secrets about this ad. One, the severity of the leak was a bit exaggerated. Poetic license. Second, half of the ad cost was subsidized by the insurance agent Bill mentions by name in the ad. But what's important here is that he recognized and capitalized on a golden opportunity, and used it as believable reason for a big sale.

Sweepstakes Winners

Want to get past, inactive customers back into your place of business? All your customers in this week? I got this in the mail, and the headline immediately grabbed me:

FINALLY—YOU ARE A SWEEPSTAKES WINNER!

I don't know about you, but I enter all those darned magazine company sweepstakes. I go for the *Reader's Digest* sweepstakes and I buy my weekly lottery tickets—after all, as a character in the movie *Let It Ride* said, "You could be walking around lucky and not know it." In a lot of years, though, I have gone winless. The guys with the balloons and the giant-sized check have not shown up at my door. So the headline FINALLY—YOU ARE A SWEEPSTAKES WINNER! got me. I read that letter. And if you send a letter to every one of your customers with that headline on it, every one of them will read it.

What should the letter say? Here's an example, courtesy of the late, great copywriter, my friend Gary Halbert:

Dear Valued Customer:

   I am writing to tell you that your name was entered into a drawing here at my store and you have won a valuable prize.

As you know, my store, ABC Jewelry, specializes in low-cost, top-quality diamond rings and diamond earrings. Well, guess what? The other day we got in a small shipment of fake diamonds that are made with a new process that makes them look so real they almost fooled me!

Anyway, I don't want to sell these fakes because they could cause a lot of trouble for the pawnbrokers around town. So I've decided to give them away to some of my good customers whose names were selected at random by having my wife, Janet, put all the names in a jar and pull out the winners.

So, you're one of the winners—and all you've got to do is drop in sometime before 5:00 P.M. Friday and you'll have a 1-karat "diamond" that looks so good it'll knock your eyes out!

Sincerely,
John Jones

P.S.: After 5:00 P.M. Friday, I reserve the right to give your prize to someone else. Thank you.

With some variation of this idea, you can get all your customers to flood your store within a short period of time. Then, if you have new products or special offers ready and waiting, the cash register will ring happily.

The Red-Tag Sale

"It's inventory clearance time and we're closing all day Friday to go through the stores and place new red tags on as many items as possible, each with the lowest price ever offered on it. Only a certain number of each red-tag item will be available, on a first-come, first-satisfied basis. The red-tag sale starts at 10:00 A.M. Saturday morning. Red tags will disappear all day long. The later in the day, the fewer the red tags."

That's the basic pitch for a red-tag sale. These tend to work well once or twice a year for retail businesses.

Coupons, Double Coupons, and Checks

Lots of people buy the newspaper on certain days just to get all the grocery store and manufacturers' coupons inside. They carefully go through all this coupon-driven advertising and inserts, scissors in hand, with buying on their minds. You can capitalize on this with an ad or insert on this day that is made up of coupons and looks like all the other coupon advertising.

If I had a shoe store, for example, my Sunday newspaper insert might be a page of coupons: one for boys' shoes, one for girls' shoes, one for men's, etc.

There's usually at least one supermarket in each area that advertises a "Double Coupon Day," when all manufacturers' coupons are accepted and doubled; a fifty-cent-off coupon becomes worth one dollar off.

If you accept manufacturers' coupons, this is a promotion worth considering. If not, there may be another way you can use the same idea. You might, for example, send a letter to your customer list in advance of your coupon-type newspaper ad advising them of its impending appearance and giving them a card or certificate that doubles the value of the coupons.

I saw a fast-food chain put up signs outside all its stores while Burger King, its competitor, was running a big coupon promotion:

WE ACCEPT BURGER KING COUPONS AND GIVE DOUBLE VALUE!

If mailing to customers for a special sale, consider enclosing a "real" check, made out to your own store, with the customer's name on it where the signature belongs. The check is redeemable at your store but otherwise useless. There's something psychologically challenging about throwing out a check.

The Premium Makes the Difference

Find a good source for one or more very desirable, appealing premiums and you can build a surge around the "free gift" you offer.

"Gift with purchase" was invented by cosmetic industry pioneer Estée Lauder. It remains the staple of that business. Visit department store cosmetic counters and you will find just about every brand has gift with purchase offers. In the retail menswear industry, where the norm is discounts, Bill Glazer frequently relied on appealing premiums instead, for his stores and the thousands following his lead, and by doing so protected profits better and put forward more interesting promotions. Televisions and other electronics are very effective premiums, particularly around Christmas. Getaway weekend packages work well for car dealers. The most interesting one I've ever seen: a free Mustang convertible with purchase of a Rolls Royce. One outstanding source of low-cost premium merchandise is the closeout merchandise industry. This industry has its own trade shows, newspaper, and catalog companies.

Many of my clients in sales fields, such as financial advisors, insurance salespeople, real-estate agents, and business-to-business sales professionals, also use the gift-with-appointment tactic to get to the desired decision makers. Some years ago, I encouraged a sales rep for a software system for dentists to send out a prospecting letter with a toothbrush enclosed to gain attention, the letter offering a six-foot-high giant toothbrush as a gift just for twenty minutes to demo the software. He got nine appointments for every ten letters sent—and they called him!

I often advise not giving away what you sell as incentive. It risks undermining your price integrity, it may not be all that motivational—just "more of the same"—and it may cost you more than appealing premiums and gifts can be obtained for from wholesale sources. If you are going to use gift-with-appointment or gift-with-purchase a lot, it's worth fully familiarizing yourself with a wide variety of wholesale sources.

In some cases, you may be able to get appealing premiums provided to you for free. The owner of several upscale jewelry stores in one market got a local gourmet restaurant to give him $100.00 gift certificates, free, to gift-with-purchases of certain jewelry items. In return, obviously, the restaurateur got promotion to customers known to have a certain level of affluence.

Premiums can and do drive sales. They can flush customers out of the woodwork who've been inactive and encourage regular customers to buy or renew earlier than their need or buy different items or services than they usually buy. Thus, they can be used not only to create a cash flow surge but also strategically to influence and alter customer behavior.

For Glazer-Kennedy Insider's Circle™, I am often writing copy to promote our next major conference, and many Members attend regularly year after year, but it's important to get as many as possible to register early, months in advance, in order to reduce the outlay of marketing dollars and boost profits and permit logistical planning based on reality rather than guesswork. Because the same people see these promotions event after event, year after year, I'm charged with figuring out a new and different premium/bonus gift to motivate that immediate, early registration. Over the years, I've had good luck with offering fees waived for the after-event Bonus Day on a specialized topic, invitations to private receptions and photo opportunities with celebrities, an opportunity to participate in competitions, and, most recently, special "take-home blueprints" matched with every workshop session. But I'm not above also using far less valuable but more beguiling items like collector-edition souvenir logo apparel and even a Dan Kennedy bobblehead!

The "My Accountant Thinks I'm Crazy" Sale

Sometimes humor works in marketing. I've used this myself, in sale promotions for my mail-order company, and I've seen both retailers and service providers use it effectively.

A tongue-in-cheek ad or letter talks about your annoyance at your nagging, domineering, penny-pinching Scroogeish accountant; how he bullies you, pushes you around, and watches you like a hawk . . . but now that he's out of town on vacation for the week, you're going to have some fun with the wildest, most generous offers in the history of your business. . . .

Sports-Related Promotions

America loves its sports activities, and sports are always on the minds of a lot of people, so tie-in promotions get favorable attention. For several years in a row, I've run a "triple-play" promotion for my mail-order company, offering a "buy one, get two free" deal to my best customers. This is the same as a 67 percent discount, but three-for-one sounds a lot bigger. And I tie the whole thing to baseball, either early in spring or at World Series time, with free baseball cards, baseball terminology and clip art, and so on. *IT'S TRIPLE PLAY TIME* has pulled as much as a 70 percent response from my customers.

Trade-Ins

Trade-in promotions are, of course, standard in the automobile business and common with sewing machines, vacuum cleaners, and automobile batteries—but there are lots of other businesses that could use this technique, including office equipment; television, stereo, and electronics; even clothing, with the trade-ins going to the Salvation Army. A spa selling memberships could accept old exercise equipment.

Easy Payment Terms

If you cover your costs, why not finance your profits? Let's say you want to feature and sell a $300.00 item that costs you $100.00. You might offer your customers this deal: $100.00 down, then four monthly payments of $50.00 each, no interest, no carrying charges. Just have them place their VISA, MasterCard, or American Express card numbers with you and sign a simple statement authorizing you to charge their credit cards each month automatically.

You can apply the same structure to hitting a certain size of purchase: buy $500.00 or more and we'll finance two-thirds of the sale.

Cash in Accumulated, Unconverted Leads

Often businesses have prospects who've called, visited websites, and even come in for appointments and not purchased who receive only a few after-the-fact attempts to persuade them to buy then are given up on. Sometimes there is a lot of dormant, untapped value there, especially if you are in a business where the purchase is likely to be a subject of procrastination due to money or timing or other reasons. At worst, periodic, aggressive marketing campaigns to old leads will usually provide enough new customers to justify the investment, but sometimes the results can be much more exciting. The following example produces between $20.00 to as much as $80.00 for every $1.00 invested in it, every time.

Great Example!

A very active Glazer-Kennedy Insider's Circle™ Member, Dr. Brian Bergh, an orthodontist, has used the following three-step direct-mail campaign for the past four years with consistent success.

This three-step letter campaign is sent to people who have had an initial consultation with Dr. Bergh for orthodontic treatment but have yet to commit to treatment. The patient or parent is given a call to action, a deadline, and a benefit for responding to the letter. This campaign offers a "birthday present" in the form of a courtesy amount off the total treatment fee as a gift from Dr. Bergh's son, Bryley. Each year, the offer has changed slightly to be relevant to Bryley's age and has been in the form of a percentage of the total fee or a hard dollar amount.

The letter sequence starts out with the first letter sent from Bryley letting the patient or parent know about the great idea he had for his birthday—to give patients in his dad's office a birthday present from him. At the end of the letter he introduces his two dogs, Rex and Scamp, as a prelude to the second and third letters that are forthcoming.

The second letter comes from the two dogs, Rex and Scamp, wondering why the patient hasn't responded yet. This letter gives the patient an excuse for being distracted and encourages him or her to take action before the deadline.

The third letter comes from one of the dogs, alluding to the fact that the patient has not responded and therefore must be lost. Sending his bigger brother, Rex, out to look for the patient didn't work, because now he's lost, too. And more drastic measures may be necessary in sending out the St. Bernard.

The first two letters are sent in colored envelopes with handwritten addresses and just a return address, no name. The third letter is sent in a brown paper bag and has a couple of dog treats included to get the extra discount. The letters are also printed on fun, festive paper to tie in with the celebration at hand.

Using children and animals appeals to many and gives Dr. Bergh an opportunity to contact patients in an appealing and fun way.

Yes, people respond to letters like this, even from a *professional* office.

Hi mister or misses,

My name is Bryley and my daddy is Dr. Bergh. He told me you came in to see him to talk about crooked teeth, but haven't done anything about it yet. My daddy says you wanted to think about getting a beautiful smile and have not decided if you want that or not.

Well, my birthday is March 23rd and I'll be six years old. I'm looking forward to taking my friend Lane to go bowling (I also want a Nintendo DS like my sister, Kaigan, has).

I told my daddy that I wanted to celebrate my 6th birthday with all his friends at his office. I thought a good way to celebrate was to have my daddy give you a present from me.

So during the month of March, my daddy will take $200 off your treatment. But since my birthday is in March, he won't be able to continue this special deal past March 31st.

Be sure to call my daddy at (818) 242-1173 today to get your present from me. Just mention my name, Bryley, for your $200 price reduction. You'll be glad you did, and so will I.

Sincerely yours,

Bryley Bergh

PS. Here are my two dogs Rex and Scamp. They were born the day after Christmas and are very fun to play with. Oh yeah, my big sister Kaigan was also born the day after Christmas.

Dr. Bergh's example: letter #1

Woof, woof;

Rex and Scamp Bergh here. We were out playing with Bryley this past weekend; he was throwing the ball for us and boy do we like to play fetch. He'd throw it and we'd run as fast as we could to get it, trying to beat each other there. Oh sorry, we just got sidetracked like we always do.

Anyway, Bryley mentioned that you hadn't called his daddy, Dr. Bergh (our great-master) for your *birthday bash discount* of $200. Bryley told us how important a beautiful and healthy smile is to you and we just can't figure out why you haven't called.

All we can figure is that you got sidetracked (like we often do) with your daily chores, work, projects, etc. We want to be sure you get the smile of your dreams, because as you know, there aren't many things more important than feeling good about yourself and being able to smile and laugh without any concerns.

Our master, Bryley, loves to smile and laugh. He also loves making people happy. We think he wants to be a clown, although he's talking about being an orthodontist just like his daddy and grand-daddy.

Be sure to call our great-master Dr. Bergh at (818) 242-1173 today to start your orthodontic treatment and receive your $200 Bryley's birthday bash discount. The deadline for this deal is quickly approaching. Bryley's birthday is March 23rd and the discount will only be good until March 31st.

Gotta go, Bryley's throwing the ball for us again. Call Dr. Bergh today at (818) 242-1173 and claim your Bryley's Birthday Bash present.

Rex and Scamp

P.S. Don't tell our great-master Dr. Bergh, but if you bring in a treat for us, Rex and Scamp, we'll make sure you get an *additional $50 off*, for a total fee reduction of $250. Just mention us, Rex and Scamp, for your gift.

Dr. Bergh's example: letter #2

Woof, woof.....woof....woof, wooooooooof,

This is Scamp and I'm really, really worried; I haven't slept for days. My great-master, Dr. Bergh, hasn't heard from you yet, and I'm worried you're lost in the Swiss Alps or someplace really far away.

I sent Rex (he's bigger than me) to look for you and now he's lost, too. I've notified Pongo and Sargeant Tibbs to start looking everywhere. I hope you're not being held hostage at Cruella DeVille's scary mansion by Horace and Jasper.

I'm going to call my friend, Bernie, the St. Bernard, right now and have him search high and low for you.

I'm also sending this first aid kit so in case you got hurt, you can fix yourself up. By the way, my great-master, Dr. Bergh, is an expert in fixing crooked and mal-aligned teeth. He knows how important it is to you to have the smile of your dreams and wants to help in any way he can.

We're still planning to celebrate Bryley's birthday on March 23rd and it won't be the same without you. Bryley's daddy is still offering $200 off your orthodontic treatment (by request of our master Bryley), and he has now agreed to honor Rex's and my last offer of an additional $50 off. You don't even have to bring in a treat for us (although we won't say no if you do) to get the extra $50 off. Just call before March 31st and I'll make sure you get that extra fee reduction – just mention my good friend Bernie.

Hoping you're OK,

Scamp

PS Be sure to call (818) 242-1173 today to claim your fee reduction of $250, **and** be sure to mention my friend, Bernie!!

Dr. Bergh's example: letter #3

What Do You Need for the Ultimate Cash Flow Surge Plan?

You've seen it all here. Ideally, you have a good list of present, active, past, maybe lost customers, and possibly a list of unconverted leads—prospects who've expressed interest, visited your store, attended your free event, and gotten information from your website but not purchased. Next, you need to construct the most compelling and appealing offer that you can. Remember to attach a satisfactory reason why. Definitely consider use of premiums. Put together a multistep, multimedia campaign to carry the offer to the list(s).

Profitably Using Marketing Technologies and Online/Internet Marketing Media

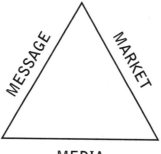

MESSAGE

MARKET

MEDIA

No Ultimate Marketing Plan could be complete without making profitable use of the current technology (which exists and is proliferating to speed up and automate the delivery of your marketing messages) and at least integrating some use of the Internet and all of its media. The key word in all of that is *profitable*. That must be your watchword. There is enormous temptation to use technology just because it exists and you can or because all the cool kids are using it, but you are a businessperson and now a savvy marketer, so you must demand each and every technology earn its way with measurable, provable profits. There is enormous pressure to be everywhere, use everything, and keep expanding your use of the Internet and all its wonders, even as each category has a wildly multiplying population. Not long ago, as example, social media was MySpace. Now it is Facebook, Twitter, LinkedIn, StumbleUpon, Reddit, and on and on and on, and it has many spreading their attention thinner and thinner and thinner desperately trying to be active in every such place. But you are a businessperson and now a savvy marketer, so you must demand each and every online media, place, and activity earn its way with measurable, provable profits. You must insist on "Show me the money!"

I begin with two confessions. One, I detest the Internet *personally* and stubbornly refuse to have anything to do with it. I happen to believe it is an extremely dangerous evil that the Pandora of technology foolishly let out of its box and that despite the enormous opportunities it brought and brings and wealth it has created and is creating, it is still far more destructive to the economy and to society than it's worth. It is the first industrial/technological revolution to erase far more jobs and small businesses than it creates, at a dramatically accelerating pace, making it the driving force (hardly anyone acknowledges) in the making of a permanent 10 to 15 percent unemployed and larger underemployed underclass and a more vicious concentrator of more wealth in fewer hands than anything we've ever seen. As the whole world is sucked into smartphones, entire industries providing hundreds of thousands of jobs each are disappearing.

It is also a dumbing-down force, creating a less intelligent, less informed, less active, less healthy, and less civil population—a retreat to living in caves and communicating in grunts. I am not alone in these opinions; numerous academic experts and business realists agree.

I do not have my computers hooked up to it (I use them as typewriters) and, in fact, *personally* have no Internet connection period. I have never *personally* surfed, Googled, or purchased anything online. I *personally* have no presence on Facebook, Twitter, LinkedIn, or anywhere else online. And for the record, I also refuse to own a cell phone, and if you are at lunch or dinner with me and take yours out, I've begun the practice of yelling for the check and leaving. Rude to rude, eye for an eye. It is my conviction we have permitted technology to go from servant to master, now directing humans in reverse evolution. We have ceased growing our capabilities in favor of an ever-growing dependence on technology for even the most mundane and simple of tasks.

So, to finish this first confession, in this chapter, you are going to get Internet marketing advice and technology advice from somebody who despises just about all of it and sees it having turned a corner from assisting business and society to at least retarding it if not destroying it.

Second confession: I have made and continue to make a great deal of money as a result of marketing technology and all things online that I personally detest, and I lack the moral character to turn my back on any of these mercenary opportunities. I know a great deal more about online marketing than people familiar with my personal preferences often assume. I direct others in the use of online marketing for me, and every day I work with clients in diverse product and service categories aggressively using online media, I write a lot of marketing copy for online media, and I guide most clients into more and better use of much of the online media. I do not need to personally ever even look at any of it in order to make use of it for profit any more than I need to enter a kitchen and cook in order to eat a gourmet dinner. Nor do you. So if you happen to share my revulsion for much of it or share my Luddite status or feel aggrieved, abused, intimidated, inept, or at least uncomfortable with it, don't let that stop you from letting it be used to make a profit for you.

Let's be very clear about everything online, from a marketing standpoint. We are talking about marketing media, which is nothing less, more, or markedly different than any and every other form of marketing media. The idea that online marketing is significantly different is utter nonsense. A hammer and a drill are different to the same very limited extent that online media is different from offline media, but they are all tools that must perform virtually the same productive purpose—i.e., a construction task or a sales task—and they are wielded in much the same way. A hammer has a head, and a drill has a pointed bit. An e-mail has a subject line, and a printed sales letter has a headline—after that difference, both are identical, both share the same purposes and functions, and both are governed by exactly the same rules (outlined in this book's companion book, *The Ultimate Sales Letter*). If you ascribe vast differences to online versus offline media, you severely handicap yourself. Don't gift any of this with more magical or mysterious properties than it really has. A stone is a stone, even if painted different colors, attached to a wire and plugged into the wall, polished to a bright shine and imaginatively merchandised as a diamond you are *required* to buy, or attached to a leash and put in a box with an owners' manual and sold as a pet.

Now, I'll give you my comments about the chief forms of online media, opportunities for good use of each, and cautions about each. The speed and constancy of change online and with online media make it problematic to publish a book such as this and its lifespan without correction or change. Writing about specifics with regard to Internet marketing in a traditionally published book is a fool's endeavor. As a result, my advice is broad and general, based on reliable marketing principles and in keeping with the entirety of *The Ultimate Marketing Plan*.

Websites

You pretty much gotta have one or more, even if your utilization of it is limited to verifying your existence and (amusingly) your legitimacy. Too many consumers responding to other forms of advertising and solicitation check the advertiser's website before taking any next steps for you to be absent. Beyond that, there are many very good reasons to have and use and possibly invest effort and/or money in driving traffic to websites. You may have reason for a brochure-type site that tells your entire business story, gives visitors a lot of freedom to roam, and is not all or predominately about directly making a sale; a site that is an online catalog; a site that is a single sales letter with a single, focused outcome; a lead-capture site that functions as kin to an 800-number and automated capture by robot voice of the interested person's contact information (and does nothing more); and a variety of customer service sites in addition to marketing sites. Customer service sites might include membership sites and informational/educational sites for specific products or services. Most business should have more than one website.

The best things about websites are the fact that an unlimited amount of real estate is fundamentally free and they can be made navigable, with their own search functions.

My favorite marketing use of websites for clients is integrated with offline media, with the offline in front of or behind the site, or both.

For example, I have a client very profitably mailing postcards to prospects on rented mailing lists of buyers of analogous products; the postcards drive the responders to a website where their contact information is captured and they can view a brief, introductory video. Those prospects are then mailed elaborate sales packages with long sales letters to sell the pricey product. In this case, the website is sandwiched in the middle of offline media and used very simply for automated contact information capture. Another client, with a chain of specialty stores, again uses direct mail, print, Valpak, as well as online search engine optimization and paid banner ads to drive people to a website offering choices of five video presentations about five different products plus a rolling-deadline coupon for the product presented in the chosen video and an automated six-step follow-up e-mail sequence.

One caution: Several different tests I personally conducted or was intimately privy to, as I was completing this book, tested offline advertisements and direct mail offering a website as the only means of response versus offering choices of a website and phone number to call. In every such test, reaching age targets as low as thirty-five, the website-only offer was far, far, far outperformed by the web and phone offer. In one instance, targeting affluent consumers over the age of fifty, the web-plus-phone pulled 300 percent more responses than the web only, and the 200 percent bump coming from offering phone proved to be of superior quality as well—measured by the prospects' stated income and net worth and by their purchases.

I take no joy from these results, despite my confessed, personal anathema toward the Internet. As a marketer, I would rather be able to offer website-only marketing and eliminate hordes of inbound telemarketers and their wages, commissions, health benefits, and managerial costs and replace them with the entirely automated technology. Also, I can do more with a lead captured online than a lead responding by phone, providing less information. So I take no joy in the *fact* that, in 90 percent of situations, it is a huge financial mistake to make visiting a website the only way an interested consumer can respond to your marketing—or, for that matter, the only way established customers can interact with you beyond their first transaction. And if you are young and of the mind that everybody cheerfully uses the Internet, polling data as recent as late 2010 revealed that 21 percent of the American public has yet to even once access or use the Internet. Assume they are all toothless, shoeless, clueless, impoverished seniors living in trailers in rural Arkansas at your extreme peril.

By this caution, I do not mean to discourage use of marketing websites. I only want to emphasize they should not be replacements (yet) for other media or for other means of consumer response.

At Glazer-Kennedy Insider's Circle™, you'll find extensive use of all kinds of online media, but specific to websites there are three primary ones: *NoBSBooks.com* is a presentation site (only) about all my books and a place readers can access extra resources related to the books. *DanKennedy.com* is the main, multipurpose institutional site presenting the company as a whole, offering newsletter subscriptions and trial subscriptions, as well as providing different access to different resources for Members at different levels. Third, *DanKennedy.com/store* takes visitors directly to the online catalog. There are also hundreds of FreeGiftFrom<Insert-Name>.com sites and variations thereof, presenting different free information, free "teaser" product, and free trial membership offers directly and through affiliates. These are single-purpose, focused sites, essentially video-supported sales letters that make direct offers. You can see an example by accepting the free invitation at the back of this book. In addition to all this, there is also *http://nobstv.dan kennedy.com*, where an online TV show featuring interviews with business and marketing experts airs. I suggest visiting all these sites to see what we're up to.

As I was writing this, the most frequently used, successful, and important strategy at many sites intended to capture contact information from new prospective customers is the double- or triple-squeeze page, so named because its purpose is to squeeze as much information as possible out of the visitor, to enable as much follow-up as possible. The first squeeze page has the lowest threshold, asking only for a name and e-mail address in exchange for access past a locked door, viewing of a video, attending a webinar, or getting free information delivered electronically. The second squeeze page, appearing after the first is successfully navigated, offers some gift or product or other physical thing sent by mail, UPS, or Federal Express, thus requiring the person's full physical address and phone number. The third, appearing after the second is successfully completed, may be a survey or questionnaire collecting information enabling the marketer to segment these prospects in some way—by interest, income, age, type of business, etc.—to facilitate customized product offerings and follow-up. The most successful marketers go to considerable extent to build lists of prospects for follow-up marketing and then to do complex, multistep, multimedia follow-up marketing. With many of my clients, we are creating first-transaction income from website visitors captured as long as two years ago.

Online Marketing Platforms

Two big, universal moneymaking principles: In discussions of wealth, such as those in my book *No B.S. Wealth Attraction in the New Economy*, I make the point that money is always in motion, and it's beneficial to be where it is moving toward, preferably positioned right in its path. Second principle: OPC, which stands for Other Peoples' Customers, is capital just like OPM, Other Peoples' Money. If you combine them, you want to be where someone else has already collected the customers you want and then engineer a way to step into the traffic of those customers as they move about and spend their money at that other person's place. In many respects, OPC is even better than OPM, as it starts you further along toward your objectives. If you amass or borrow capital, you must then invest it—and put it at risk—in finding, attracting, and purchasing customers. It's faster and surer to skip all that and start with customers.

Using Video

YouTube is not just a giant bazaar of TV clips and funny videos—it is the second-largest search engine, trailing only Google. YouTube offers an opportunity for you to promote your business, and all you need—technically—is an inexpensive flip-video camera or Kodak Zi8 pocket camcorder. You can produce your own videos and upload to YouTube.
—from Rick Gee, *www.MarketingProfitStrategiesblog.com*

An additional resource to check out regarding video is *www.The VideoMarketingGuru.com*.

A marketing platform is a place where customers already gather and also a place or media that allows you to promote yourself and your wares to those customers. Offline, a good example would be the artist who secures a spot on a cruise ship during a ten-day cruise, where he gets to have a reception, showing, and art auction one evening; promote it over the ship's loudspeaker system every morning leading up to it; have invitations distributed to all the staterooms; and after the event have a gallery location. The ship is his marketing platform. And in the offline, physical world you should look for and take advantage of as many appropriate platforms as you can.

Online, just about anybody's website visited or patronized by the same customers you seek could be a marketing platform for you, but there are a number of big, commercial platforms with formal ways of using them—notably eBay, Amazon, and Google, Google AdWords, and Google Shopping. Most people know about eBay, but not as many people are familiar with the opportunities to open their own online store at Amazon or the opportunities to use Google Shopping. Very recently, the owner of a very small specialty store in my neighborhood told me he'd been getting five or six sales a week from his website for over a year and thought of it as a nice little bonus over and above his local business, but immediately after connecting to Google Shopping, he began averaging over fifty online sales a week. A client of mine in the nutrition business is taking in over $20,000.00 a month from her store on Amazon's platform. She also cleverly wrote and self-published several health books that she sells at nominal prices via Amazon, with the books all ending with sales letters for her bee pollen–based supplements.

Google in totality is the biggest platform, but with its size comes bureaucracy, arbitrariness, and outright stupidity that frustrates and frightens many marketers. I have a client making well over $100,000.00 a month entirely from new customers generated from Google, including SEO activity (search engine optimization), spending on Google AdWords, and using Google Shopping—but rather than basking in the glow of his prosperity, he is racing to liberate himself from dependency on Google because, as he puts it, he has trouble sleeping at night knowing his entire destiny is in the hands of a corporate monster. He is well-served by his paranoia and active pursuit of diversity, but the power of Google AdWords and SEO on Google can't be ignored. The two leading authorities helping marketers use and maximize results from Google AdWords happen to be Glazer-Kennedy Insider's Circle™ Members, and they are happy to be of help to readers of this book. If you are already investing $5,000.00 or more on Google AdWords or are capable of such investment, I urge contacting Timothy Seward at *www.ROIRevolution.com* and arranging for a free AdWords Optimizer Strategy Consulting Call. If you are a smaller player, in need of solid do-it-yourself strategies for Google, I urge contacting my friend Perry Marshall, author of the book *Definitive Guide to Google AdWords,* at *www.perrymarshall.com.*

For every one of these major platforms, there are how-to books available, written by people who began using them for their businesses, grew big incomes with them, and made themselves into experts on their use. A simple visit to a bookstore or an online bookseller will get you to them. Most of these entities also have online tutorials and other assistance for new merchant-users as well.

This is an ideal way for a local business to expand its reach with little outlay of cash or risk, and it may lead you to an even bigger opportunity than your present business.

Another kind of platform that sprung to life right around the same time I was writing this book is the "deal of the day" media, where somebody has assembled a large opt-in list of consumers, by local area or by special interest, who welcome a daily or weekly e-mail offering of a great deal, bargain, or discount from a local or specialty merchant. The lion in this jungle when I wrote this was Groupon.com, but many others were racing to adapt or improve on its model. Among them are LivingSocial and, by the direct-mail coupon mailer Valpak, Valpak Deals. Groupon members are not just directed to the merchant offering the deal; they buy the discount vouchers upfront, from Groupon, guaranteeing a high rate of redemption. Groupon was in fourteen local markets at inception and, in one year's time, was operating in over 300 local markets spanning thirty-one countries. A number of Glazer-Kennedy Insider's Circle™ Members and a couple of clients have reported success, to varying degrees, marketing their business via Groupon. The price of acquiring customers via a third-party coupon seller like Groupon is high. Not only is the merchant giving a discount of 60 to 70 percent or equivalent exceptional value, they are sharing revenue with the coupon seller like Groupon and they do not have access to the database of the coupon buyers—only those who redeem them. Still, in many cases, the true, total cost of acquiring new customers directly is as high or higher, and the speed of acquisition slower.

In the specialty interest category, I have a client, KidsBowlFree.com, which markets for bowling centers to over 1 million families online, but is expanding with paid marketing for other kid- or family-oriented businesses to that same opt-in list of families. These online marketing entities are in the same position traditional mail-order catalog companies are in that they have active, responsive lists of people looking to them to bring forward relevant, interesting, value-priced products, services, and offers—so they *need* new products, services, and offers or they risk losing the valuable relationship they have with their list. These online entities, almost without exception, make their money from fees and/ or revenue sharing with merchants, not from the consumers on their lists, so they also *need* merchants with hot products or offers that a large number of the people on their lists will buy. (See advice in Chapter 2 concerning irresistible offers.)

I encourage active, aggressive, continuous exploration of all these platform opportunities. Good access to already assembled and qualified potential customers or, better yet, already assembled, actual customers with a proven willingness to spend money on products and services closely analogous to yours is one of the single most beneficial strategies you'll ever use.

Social Media

Almost everything that sustains existence on the Internet starts out as one thing and rather quickly evolves into another, with that evolution often including a transition from having no profit-making model and only the ambition and purpose of aggregating traffic at its inception to a real business required to generate revenue and make a profit. Amazon began as an online bookseller; it's now one of the world's largest merchants of just about everything. In 2010, Amazon paid $545 million to buy Diapers.com, Soap.com, and Beauty-Bar.com, and that's just one of many demonstrations of its commitment by creation and by acquisition to become the biggest seller and product distribution platform of everything. Jeff Bezos, the founder of Amazon, could be cast as a Bond villain bent on world domination. eBay began as an online swap meet but expanded into the auction business, a closeout merchandise distribution channel for brand-name retailers and manufacturers (somewhat mimicking the outlet malls that dot the physical landscape), and keeps trying to make itself about even more. Both of these also, as described previously, became the media for other merchants and marketers and are in the merchant services businesses.

Facebook began as a way for friends to communicate and for people to make new friends. It was the small-town gatherings at church, hardware store, and high school game brought online. This incarnation lasted about sixty seconds. Celebrities were among the first to figure out how it could be used for commercial purposes. Comedian Dane Cook, now well known in the stand-up comedy business, built his fan base almost entirely via Facebook. Comedians are able to drive their fans to their club appearances, authors are able to drive book sales, and actors and movie studios promote films via Facebook. Today, it is very much a business marketing media and platform, with Facebook sites designed to flip traffic to websites that sell products and services. Facebook itself began aggressively offering marketing services for fees, utilizing data harvested from users, and engineering campaigns to selected users. Given that four to six months will pass between my writing this book and you having the opportunity to read it, it's a safe wager that the range of direct advertising and marketing opportunities Facebook will be selling will have greatly expanded.

This same movement from a gathering of friends or a gathering of people with a special interest to a fully commercialized advertising, marketing, and selling media rife with opportunities for local and global merchants exists with Twitter, YouTube, and (if not now, will in the near future) every similarly structured online activity site. Kim Kardashian's last round of TV commercials for a hamburger chain were supported by her tweets to her Twitter list and communiqués to her Facebook fans, driving millions to watch premieres of the commercials at YouTube, and the size and activity of her social media lists influenced the company's choosing and hiring her as their celebrity du jour and the amount they were willing to pay her. Even game-playing sites like Farmville inevitably morph into ad media. In 2010, Farmville hosted its first major marketing event for a big corporation: McDonald's. It won't be the last.

In short, the term "social media" is mythical.

Real social media is a neighborhood potluck with no commercial agenda or sponsors, bringing neighbors who may not know each other together, facilitating new friendships and creating an environment for purely social conversation. This is basically what businesses like Facebook and Twitter want to be seen as, but it's definitely *not* what they are. The CEO of Tupperware Brands, Rick Goings, one of the smartest marketers and CEOs that I know, told me that they thought of it all as *anti*social media, as it was actually more isolating of individuals than it was a force of legitimate socialization. Nonetheless, Tupperware does make extensive use of it—but has never dreamt of attempting to replace their *real* social media (home parties and, for agents, sales meetings) with it.

Many users of social media sites prefer and participate in the mass delusion that they are engaged in social activity with friends, but the reality is these sites are businesses all about selling goods and services. You will hear from both users and "experts" in social media that there is resistance to the commercialization, that you may offend a lot of inhabitants of these online places by being too overtly commercial, that there is a noncommercial culture there to be sensitive to—and that's all hooey.

Here's a simple rule that has made me millions and kept me from wasting a lot of time and energy: *If I can't sell, I don't go.*

In this case, there's a ton of selling going on, at an ever-increasing pace and pervasiveness. Do not let yourself be intimidated about selling. Find every way you can to use these media to sell, and resist any pressure to use them for other purposes.

To be encouraging rather than discouraging, here's a social media marketing success story from a very ordinary business, given to me by my friends Dean Killingbeck and Mark Ijlal, authors of the book *FULL: A Complete Online & Offline Roadmap to Marketing Your Restaurant.* Two partners with a mobile taco stand selling Korean BBQ tacos from a kitchen truck were struggling in the cluttered, competitive, urban market of Los Angeles. Their business breakthrough came from Twitter. One partner began broadcasting the truck's locations, times there, and descriptions of unique food items on Twitter, in advance and in real time, hour by hour. They also encouraged their happy customers to tweet while enjoying their tacos, to spread the word. Their follower list grew exponentially, from 10 followers to 100 to 500 to 5,000. Their truck was soon mobbed at every stop, and a second truck was added. As of this writing, they have four trucks "fed" by 74,000 followers on Twitter. If you happen to own a restaurant (or similar business) and you'd like some **free help** from Dean and Mark on the use of Twitter, visit *www.TheFullRestaurantBook.com/ActionPlan* and click on the Twitter-related buttons.

E-Mail Marketing

E-mail marketing is extremely seductive because it has nominal or no cost. Truth is, bargains in marketing are rare and incidental. For the most part, you get what you pay for. If buying 200 radio spots at one station costs $20,000.00 and another costs $2,000.00, neither is probably a better bargain than the other; factoring quantity and quality of audiences, you're probably paying the same amount per set of qualified ears. Same with everything else, including e-mail and the comparison of it to regular mail or telemarketing or other media. However, I don't believe any of this should be looked at in either-or terms but rather in multimedia terms, as complementary multimedia, integrated media relationships. I would never advise a client to use only e-mail and never send "snail mail"—that is criminally stupid and an utterly false bargain, for so many firmly evidenced reasons there's no room here to enumerate them. On the other hand, given the nominal cost, it's pretty damn dumb not to integrate e-mail into follow-up or front-end marketing.

The unrivaled leaders in both knowledge about e-mail marketing and the implementation of e-mail marketing as well as sophisticated multimedia follow-up marketing for any kind and size of business are my friends Clate Mask and Scott Martineau, founders of the e-mail marketing/marketing software system company Infusionsoft and authors of a book you must read: *Conquer the Chaos.* For all Infusion System users combined, they send about 500 million e-mails per calendar quarter (!!!), with a remarkable deliverability success rate of 98 percent, achieved in an environment where deliverability is a severe problem. Over 55 percent of brand-new Infusion users successfully get at least two marketing campaigns featuring e-mail implemented within their first sixty days. If you want to be able to fully capitalize on both e-mail marketing in general and superior follow-up on prospects, you should investigate all the help Infusion offers. You can get **free information at** *www.ConquerTheChaosbook.com*, and you can see Infusionsoft products, services, and training demonstrated at Infusionsoft.com. If you wind up directly communicating with the folks at Infusionsoft, identify yourself as a reader of this book and ask if you can get a complimentary copy of the recording of my *No-Fail Fix-Your-Follow-Up* presentation I did at seminars sponsored by Infusionsoft.

A Few Additional Tips

There is e-mail marketing, and then there is e-mail marketing. The most overt is the simple, straightforward "Hey, we've got our best designer bags on sale this week only at up to 70% off last week's prices. Click here or come on in . . . " Nothing wrong with such simple campaigns. They drive a lot of sales for a lot of businesses, large and small. The temptation to overcomplicate them should even be resisted. I overheard a conversation, one guy telling a buddy about getting an e-mail from Dunkin' Donuts offering four one-pound bags of coffee for $19.00, less than $5.00 a pound, and that he had stopped on the way to their lunch to grab the deal before it went away. The guy's a regular Dunkin' customer, likes the coffee, buys it regularly, and welcomes their e-mail, so he required nothing cleverer than "Coffee On Sale" as an e-mail subject line and eagerly responded to a price-driven offer. You just don't need to get cute or creative with this sort of thing. If you are a Glazer-Kennedy Insider's Circle™ Gold or Diamond Member (see the back of this book), you get these exact kind of "sale of the week" opportunities by simple, straightforward e-mail—for different resources from our catalog, new resources, and occasionally other publishers' resources—most weeks, all year long.

More sensitive is the development of a prospect not yet a customer, through e-mail follow-up after they have visited your website or otherwise expressed interest and open-mindedness but haven't bought anything. Here, one very effective strategy is the delivery of a home study course in short e-mail installments—one lesson every day or every other day over one, two, or several weeks. Every product or service is the basis for subject matter, so I've crafted these for chiropractors, dentists, hearing aid centers, financial advisors, wedding and event planners, photography studios, skin care and acne treatment product marketers, and on and on. By having the prospect enroll in a consumer education course rather than agree to getting e-mail from you, your own positioning is improved, the likelihood of the e-mails being opened and read leaps up, and the credence given the content of the e-mails improves as well.

Last, be sensitive to age-related preferences and consumers' expressed preferences with regard to e-mail versus snail mail. My daughter, who is in the forty-year-old neighborhood, is perfectly happy receiving e-mail birthday cards and thinks no less of them or their senders than she does of the people sending actual cards from Hallmark. My wife, however, a few handfuls of years older, is always *disappointed* by the e-mail greetings. If you include the sending of birthday greetings in your ongoing customer relationship nurturing, as part of your Ultimate Marketing Plan, surely you don't want to get a disappointed reaction, do you? You would be better served doing nothing at all. Thus, you would age segment your customer list, and treat different segments differently. This is a simple example with far-reaching implications.

Other Marketing Technology—Old Reliables

Broadcast fax is an old standby taken away by law from U.S. marketers operating within the United States, with a few exceptions, such as membership associations communicating with their own members with their express and periodically renewed permission. However, in Canada, the United Kingdom, and many other countries, mass broadcast faxing even to prospects with whom you have no prior relationship is still perfectly permissible. It is a powerful B2B marketing tool. It is intrusive and hard to ignore, has immediacy and urgency, and can be graphically eye-catching and intriguing. And it's dirt-cheap.

Advertised "free recorded messages," sometimes presented as "consumer information hotlines," are appealing to many prospective customers you've aroused curiosity or interest in but who are fearful of calling for information and being harangued by a telesales shark, and who are much more prone to respond by phone than going to a website or who are listening to a radio commercial while driving or otherwise in a situation where responding immediately needs to be easy and non-threatening. For many years, pre-Internet, the offer of a free recorded message as an alternative means of response and a "baby step" for the intrigued prospect played a major role in the advertising and marketing I did for clients in almost every type of business. Hundreds of thousands of small-business owners following my lead on this discovered that simply adding an option of calling and hearing a free consumer awareness message, with an intriguing title as a recorded message, significantly bumped response and return on investment from their Yellow Pages ads, print ads in other media, Valpak coupons, and direct mail. With the advent of websites, the majority of advertisers have abandoned the use of this tool—foolishly! It is never smart to be seduced by newly popular media tools to the extent that you leave others that are working for you behind. In marketing, you're legally allowed as many "wives" as you like. Don't jilt or abandon any. You don't need to trade one in for the other. I remain a fan, advocate, and strategic user of free recorded messages.

Two of my long-time clients not only made their own businesses infinitely more successful with the use of free recorded messages, but they went on to revolutionize their respective industries by teaching thousands of their peers to use them. In real estate, Craig Proctor became and for many years stayed one of the top RE/MAX agents in the entire world with the advertising of free recorded messages as fuel. In the carpet cleaning industry, Joe Polish liberated cleaning company operators from cheap-price and free-room advertising by teaching them to sell based on expertise and consumer education, with free recorded messages as the primary tool. There is no good reason not to use these strategies and this tool today, particularly if your target market is fifty or sixty years of age or older, or resistant to Internet use and giving contact information via websites.

Automated lead capture by recorded message is also alive, well, and useful, cost-efficient especially if bringing in a lot of leads, and sometimes more effective than having calls taken "live" by humans. Automated answering gives you 24/7 coverage, zero human errors by operators, and a nonthreatening environment for the caller. There are many companies providing these services, but a leader in the field is Automated Marketing Solutions, which you can check out at *www .automatedmarketingsolutions.com.*

Finally, with Alexander Graham Bell's little invention, there is **voice broadcast**, meaning the mass, instantaneous delivery of a canned message to hundreds, thousands, or even millions of phone numbers. For a time, this was a widely, creatively, and very profitably used marketing media. A major trucking company used voice broadcast to recruit new drivers, which gave me the idea to employ it for cold prospecting for a client company in network marketing to recruit new distributors, and over 20,000 prospects were created this way every month. The president of Glazer-Kennedy Insider's Circle™, Bill Glazer, in his first business— an extremely successful menswear store—used celebrity-impersonator-voiced broadcasts (featuring Elvis, President Bill Clinton, and many others) and seasonally timed blasts to promote sales to thousands of customers. One of his best was done himself, timed for delivery precisely at midnight on New Year's Eve, with full-bore party noise in the background. Sadly, the Do Not Call Registry law virtually wiped out the ability to use this marvelous technology for reaching out to new prospects with whom you have no relationship, but it can still be used, carefully, with established customers from whom you have permission on file for communication by telephone. Despite this fact, its use has nearly ended as business owners have moved to e-mail. Big mistake. E-mails are easily ignored. A message in your voice mail, wedged between the message from your ne'er-do-well brother-in-law asking to borrow money and your neighbor apologizing for his dog's latest destruction of your garden is not so easily ignored.

Other Marketing Technology—New, Fast Changing, and Experimental

It is impractical for a book like this to address the newest, fast-developing tech media, particularly those for which the jury is still out about its sustainability and true effectiveness. Some marketing technologies prove short-lived for many different reasons. I lived through a relatively brief boom for 900-numbers, during which books were pumped out, seminars held, gurus anointed, services sold, peer pressure to use intense, and a stampede to use achieved—yet it was all over within a hurry. More recently, there was a similar gold rush to Internet radio. For a short while, it was The Next Big Thing every marketer was talking about and many of my clients were enthralled with. As I write this, the bloom is off this rose for many, and more are more fascinated with Internet television.

As I write this, marketing through mobile devices is the hottest new trend. Creating apps, text messaging, delivery of voice messages to cell phones, and other direct-to-smart-devices communication are all being hastily embraced by marketers large and small, with results varying widely. Some of this will sort itself out in just a matter of months, some will go away in short order, some may develop into a staple.

In its totality, technology and tech media gives you, the marketer, opportunities, advantages, and hazards.

One great opportunity is to reach prospects and customers in new ways and possibly reach people via one of these ways you might not reach otherwise. Another great opportunity is to be more diverse, expansive, and aggressive in marketing with relatively low-cost media. The biggest advantage is that tech media tends to democratize marketing opportunity, to level the playing field between the well-capitalized Goliaths and the tiniest Davids. After all, a tweet is a tweet, and McDonald's really can't do it any better or any differently than can the two partners with the Korean BBQ taco truck. For these reasons, you have to pay attention, seek information, learn, evaluate, assess, and choose to use at least some of it in some ways.

The hazards are severe. The biggest is becoming too easily distracted and seduced, chasing after one shiny object after another but never really locking in a foundational Ultimate Marketing Plan you stick with and systematically, doggedly implement with consistency and constancy. Another is permitting yourself to be overwhelmed and spread too thin trying to do too many things or, worse, everything and every new thing. You have to rank and rerank opportunities, and act realistically within the context of your resources, time, willingness to work, and willingness to learn. Better to do five marketing activities very well for maximum impact than fifty poorly with minimum impact.

Tech is incredibly seductive. Visit an Apple store on a Saturday to see its seductiveness in action. Watch how fast the masses line up to buy the next new gizmo, even if the gizmo already in hand is meeting all their needs with immense capabilities left over. Observe people abandoning thought for dependence. People use handheld GPS to direct them step by step to the nearest Starbucks. Incredible. This seductiveness extends into the small business and into the corporate boardroom so that too much behavior mimics that of the people lining up outside that Apple store at 4:00 A.M. to be in the first few thousand to get their paws on that next gadget. Distraction, diffusion of resources, and neglect or abandonment of what works are all hazards to be vigilant of.

Reality Check on Media

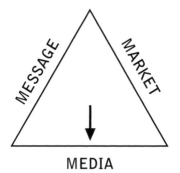

These days, many businesses struggle with too many media choices to manage, financial pressure not to use them all and to choose the cheapest, and peer pressure to favor trendy media over old media. Here are a few *facts* to add to your pondering:

Print Versus Online

A major university, not eager to be named but reporting to one of the research groups I subscribe to, was thinking about saving money by discontinuing its six-times-a-year alumni magazine and delivering it only online. A survey of alumni showed that 78 percent favored the move and indicated a preference for receiving it online. **But, 63 *percent of the donors* expressed strong disapproval** and wanted to continue receiving the printed magazine. Along the same lines, the director of an animal rescue charity told me that their print newsletter always generated more in immediate donations than it cost, brought donations from people who never responded to their e-mail campaigns, and, in 2009, brought in over a dozen new big donors—me included. And, like me, most had been receiving it for many months before writing the first check.

(*Source:* EPMCOM.com, research services. Non-Profit & Charitable Fundraising Report, 2009)

Still Using Mail

If you're used to your mailbox stuffed with catalogs, you've undoubtedly noticed a reduction in bulk and frequency. However, few successful mail-order companies have abandoned print catalogs—most have just gotten better at list management. Frederick's of Hollywood, for example, is building more "value offers" into its catalogs, putting two or three items together in "buy 2, get 1 free" packages, then *mailing more* **catalogs** to its better customers. The formula is better offers to better customers by proven media. To their credit, they did *not* respond to sales headwinds by refusing to build better offers or by discontinuing use of the media that has supported them so well in favor of cheaper choices.

Another cataloguer, SimplySoles, merchandiser of high-priced designer shoes, has added lower-priced bags, jewelry, and other accessories; promoted pairings of items in its catalogs; and reports that their catalog "has had the best performance (in 2010) in 3 years." Sprint, a company providing cell-phone service and with an obvious ability to communicate with its customers via texts to drive online, is using direct mail profitably to promote loyalty and referral programs, and it sends a new-customer welcome package *by mail*, and a newsletter *by mail*. They also give each member a personalized website where they can monitor use, modify plans, and redeem rewards, but they are **communicating with customers for retention** *by mail.*

(*Source:* DM NEWS 5-17-10)

Reality Check on Social Media As *Marketing* Media

Okay, so *everybody* is tweeting friends and family and uploading their entire lives to Facebook and is obsessed with it all. And *everybody* in business is devoting their lives to using it as a marketing media. One of the types of small businesses I've believed was using social media profitably was restaurants. But, here are the results from *Nation's Restaurant News'* annual survey of restaurant customers and restaurant owners, which this year asked about social media. Look at the remarkable differences . . .

- **Only 8 percent** of consumers follow a restaurant on Facebook, but 61 percent of restaurant owners have a Facebook site and do active Facebook marketing for their business.
- **Only 15 percent of consumers** anticipate following more restaurants on Facebook, but 78 percent of the restaurant owners have plans to increase their use of it as a marketing tool.
- **Only 3 percent** pay attention to a restaurant or restaurants via Twitter, while 53 percent of restaurants use Twitter for marketing purposes.
- **Only 9 percent** expect to use Twitter more regarding restaurants they patronize, while 66 percent of restaurants intend doing more with Twitter.
- More than one-third of the consumers surveyed are younger than age thirty-five.

What can be made of this? Years back, I consulted with a chain of clinics spending 80 percent of its ad budget on the Yellow Pages but, when pressed to track, found less than 15 percent of its patients coming from there. Nearly 60 percent came from referrals, on which they spent less than 5 percent of the budget encouraging, incentivizing, and rewarding, and 15 percent came from radio, which they were on the verge of discontinuing. To be entirely fair, the 8 percent who follow their favorite restaurants may very well be such high-value, exceptionally responsive customers that committing greatly disproportionate resources to it *may* be wise—but you'd better be very aware of the ratio.

I have an idea. Try it out. Let it roll around.

Resources should be earned by and allocated in proportion to performance.

Resources might mean prime shelf space in a supermarket, advertising dollars, the sales manager's coaching, leads distributed to salespeople, or time spent on social media.

Resources should be *earned by* performance.

The old Physicians Weight Loss operating principle regarding their inbound telemarketers was three strikes and you're out; take three calls, fail to schedule any appointments, and you are fired—next batter up. 'Cuz each call costs money to get. If it's only 8:20 A.M. on Monday, your first day on the job, and you started at 8:00, it doesn't matter. You're out. Next.

Resources should be *allocated in proportion to* performance.

I have a client famous for its TV advertising and thought of by most as a TV advertiser, but over the past three to five years, they have quietly shifted more and more dollars away from TV into print and direct mail as evidence has shown the total return on investment is better with customers acquired by these means. They would *prefer* using only TV. More TV.

Extension of this idea: Black holes cannot be permitted to consume resources. No, never stop testing and retesting regardless of past performance because most facts do change. But you can't let yourself be where the restaurant owners likely are, overinvesting attention, time, and money and increasing that investment disproportionately to social media's actual performance and their customers' use of it *as means of making buying decisions*. You can't get confused about the goal here. It's not how many friends or fans the tavern has on Facebook; it's how many customers it has in it drinking and eating every night.

(Source: *2010 NRN/Channel Marketing Survey. NRN.com)

Watch Your ROI

Lest you get the wrong lesson: I am *not* opposed to any marketing media. None. I am a financial pragmatist very capable of divorcing personal preference from these kinds of choices and decisions, as you need to be. I am no more or less against *anti*social media than I am against paid displays of logos and websites as tattoos on boxer's foreheads or bikini bottoms of babes playing beach volleyball. It all has moral equivalency in my book. I just want to **clearly see and account for the return on investment, then make the next week's investment choices based on hard data, on harsh reality, and proportionate to each media's contribution to sales and, ideally, net profit.**

I *have* preferences, but I do *not* indulge them as investor anymore than I choose the horse to bet on in a race based on which driver I like best or least personally. There are entire businesses I choose, and am fortunate in being able to choose to eschew based on preference—but in a business, my enthusiasm or lack thereof for any particular media or methodology is earned. So don't go discrediting the facts of the above survey nor my comments based on the presumption I'm indulging personal bias. I take no joy in finding failure in any media; I'd rather another new one was invented every day and they all performed well and equally well, so we could all make even more money. I would rather pizza burned off calories, dogs were calibrated to die the exact same minute as their owners, and Johnny Carson was still the host of *The Tonight Show*.

I have even, very recently, personally spent about $25,000.00 on media and its use that I am fervently skeptical of because professionals I respect made a compelling case and I am willing to test *against* my own instincts (honed over thirty years in direct marketing)—and I hope have my expectations proven wrong and such big ROI demonstrated that I will make much use of this for myself and my clients. Could I be wrong? Sure—that's why I've taken $25,000.00 out of my pocket to find out. Will I be proven wrong? Sadly, I doubt it. If I can, I'll let you know. But I know the mind, like the parachute, is most valuable *open*. So don't just write my curmudgeonly cautions about new media off as biased. And specific to restaurants, I'll be happy to share a Member's fact-based report of profitable use of the social media that belies the NRN survey.

Specific to fundraising, if 65 percent of the donors had preferred online, I'd have told you. Regardless of that, the point, the principle remains: Guard your money and time against individual or mass delusion, blindly following popular fads or false prophets or seductive fiction, and **insist on evidence.** Invest prudently. **Be an independent thinker.**

Resources

Here is a list of some of the smartest pencils in the tech media marketing box that will provide complimentary resources for readers of this book.

- Russell Brunson, extraordinarily effective websites:
  www.russellbrunson.com*
- Bill Glazer, online marketing and publishing:
  www.DanKennedy.com*
- Frank Kern, Internet marketer extraordinaire:
  www.frankkern.com
- Clate Mask/Scott Martineau, e-mail marketing:
  www.infusionsoft.com
- Perry Marshall, Google AdWords:
  www.perrymarshall.com
- Timothy Seward, Google AdWords:
  www.RoiRevolution.com
- Yanik Silver, online commerce and marketing:
  www.surefiremarketing.com
- Jeff Walker, online product launch specialist:
  www.jeffwalker.com

*Russell Brunson and Bill Glazer both provide current marketing advice to Glazer-Kennedy Insider's Circle™ Members on an ongoing business. See the invitation at the back of this book.

Bonus Chapters

The following two chapters showcase two business owners using most of the Ultimate Marketing Plan Success Factors in their businesses—use the lists and identify as many at work as you can. One is a consumer service business (Grant Miller's), the other a retail/food business (Diana Coutu's). I have not included a B2B example purely because of page-count limitations and a decision to show you two of the best examples I have. But do not fall victim to "But My Business Is Different" narrow-minded thinking and excuse making. By this point, you should realize that every business needs to be a marketing business and that any doing a great job at it can and should be studied and emulated, regardless of the direct similarity or dissimilarity to the deliverables in your business.

Making an Ordinary Business Unique

I was so impressed with everything I learned about Grant Miller's business, I went to see it for myself and reported on my visit in one of the Glazer-Kennedy Insider's Circle™ newsletters, the No B.S. *Marketing to the Affluent Letter*. This is a recap of that report. Grant and I spent the day together, with a tour of the flagship location of his five Sun Your Buns tanning salons, then reviewed all of his outstanding advertising and marketing materials.

As background, you should know that his home city, Erie, Pennsylvania, is fundamentally a blue-collar population center, but Grant is a premium-price marketer—his average prices are significantly higher than local competitors or national averages in his industry. In fact, his salons rank in the top dozen or so in the entire country. The five locations combined deliver over 200,000 tanning sessions per year, and business is up year to year, including in 2008 to 2009 and 2009 to 2010 in defiance of the recession.

I'm going to take you through a partial list of everything Grant does, does differently, and has in place that is making this company such a standout success, but you should also visit the website to see a lot more: *www.sunyourbuns.com*. Candidly, very few businesses (including upscale ones) actually impress me, but this one does. You will see much of *The Ultimate Marketing Plan* demonstrated, but you'll also discover additional strategies not mentioned previously in this book. The core idea, though, is to take an ordinary business that is relatively easy to commoditize and tends to battle cheap-price competition and make it unique and uniquely attractive to a chosen clientele.

Multiple Product and Price Presentations

The customer base is diverse—including very young women, even teens, to professional career women and affluent-but-not-desperate housewives, so the idea of different prices for different customers definitely applies. The business centers on monthly continuity, not per-tan purchasing, and on reoccurring revenue from members, not random revenue from walk-ins. To that end, Grant has different monthly continuity levels, each tied to a different "product" or tanning booth(s), from a no-frills, slow tan booth (think: Kia or Holiday Inn) all the way up to the most deluxe, comfortable, state-of-the-art, computer-programmed unit (think: Bentley or Ritz-Carlton). The staff presents this via a scripted and choreographed tour, showing the best first, and via a sales card (shown in this book, see Chapter 1). While new, first-time customers are brought in by many different promotions, including single-tan offers, *the* objective is conversion to membership. His product/price strategies include:

- **Tiered Pricing**: from low to very high, with membership and with ancillary products, such as lotions—which go all the way up to $100.00 a bottle.
- **Membership-Continuity**. Notable: comprehensive retention strategies, including a "put membership on hold" option (as the

business has a seasonal factor)—this allows members to pay just $5.00 a month *not* to use the facilities but keep their membership intact and avoid initiation fees when restarting. There are, at any given time, hundreds paying this fee! They form a list segment all their own, getting periodic mailing campaigns to get them to restart and come in.

- **New Packages.** Grant frequently changes things up, adding a new, improved tanning machine and creating a new package for it. As I was writing this, he'd started experimenting with a different form of membership, "Keys to the Salon," which entitles the member to use any of the different tanning booths at any time, and to unlimited use.

- **Free Trial Offers.** Many promotions feature a free trial or $1.00, $5.00, etc. trial offers. As I was writing this, he'd been experimenting with a $19.00/30-Days' Unlimited Tanning introductory offer that was bringing in better quality customers and providing better opportunity for them to get hooked on the tanning experience. You can only do these kinds of free trial offers if your sales/membership conversion process is effective.

Advertising/Marketing Media

On the following pages, I have shown you a small assortment of his advertising and marketing pieces. Grant relies very heavily on newspaper inserts and ads, Valpak, and his own solo direct mail, predominately postcards. He has mailing campaigns for present customers, past/inactive customers, and to selected neighborhoods, "farming" for new customers, all occurring very frequently. The reprints here do not do justice; most of this is printed in full color, with bold graphics, and, often, sexy photographs. Some, however, feature him, use humor, or have seasonal tie-ins. Keep in mind, this is a partial list.

- Monthly print newsletter: customers, members, lapsed members
- Postcards 1×–2× per month: different offers
- List segmentation: different lists get different offers.
- Late-in-year promotion postcard: $49.00–$79.00 Unlimited Use, balance of the year
- Rescue campaigns for membership drop-outs
- Flyers and newspaper inserts
- Valpak
- Referral request postcards + referral promotions (big-screen TV giveaway when I was there)
- Loyalty rewards
- Survey cards—for feedback and development of testimonials
- "Bounceback"/thank-you postcard—to get a nonmember back
- Birthday offer postcard
- Websites
- SEO
- Social media: YouTube, Facebook

Environment/Experience

The environment is much more like an upscale spa salon than a tanning salon with its big, open reception area, natural wood and pastel colors, and reception desk. The booths themselves are arranged in a big circle around the reception desk, each with privacy rooms. His order of arrangement (and presentation) is the polar opposite of most in his industry; his booths are arranged with the best/most expensive in front and presented first. Significantly, each room has photographs outside, in case it is in use during a tour. The entire environment is upscale, several levels above industry norms and most new customers' expectations.

As an interesting aside, this business began as an experiment, adding a few low-end, basic tanning booths to the video stores Grant owned before he developed this company. When deciding to exit the video business and commit to this industry, he decided he wanted to be able to attract and keep affluent clientele and deliver an experience vastly superior to the typical tanning salon—which is usually sterile and ordinary, typically with booths stuck in a strip center location with little improvement of the environment. Grant's salon could be installed inside a top-flight resort hotel and be right at home.

- **Comprehensive Internal Controls.** Everything is scripted, supported by checklists, and quality control is made visible to customers to impose pressure for compliance on staff; for example, the cleanliness and sanitization form that must be completed by staff after preparing a room for a customer is on a clipboard in the room, visible to the customer.
- **Full Video/Audio Surveillance—Sales Enforcement.** The main area where staff interacts with customers and sales activity occurs is under constant A/V surveillance so that Grant can eavesdrop via his laptop on any of the five locations live or after the fact. A/V surveillance is also used for noncompliance in coaching (or firing) staff. See Chapter 13 in my book *No BS Ruthless Management of People & Profits* for more. And know: What you won't enforce, you won't get.

Expansion

Entrepreneurs operate in realms of GROWTH *and* EXPANSION; most business owners only in growth. In addition to growing the core business via multiple locations, additional tanning booths/equipment, and evermore aggressive marketing to bring in customers and (targeted) to smooth over seasonal highs and lows, Grant has also expanded into nontanning products and services at the salons, opened a second business that can be cross-marketed to the same customers, and is now readying an infomarketing/coaching business for his industry. There is no standing still here.

- Laser skin rejuvenation
- Teeth whitening
- Second business (gym/fitness center)—for cross-marketing free trial offers.

The ability to stay in a mode of continuous growth and expansion is only possible for a small or even midsized company owner who has a (continuously updated) Ultimate Marketing Plan in place. Business owners who fly by the seat of their pants are so consumed by the here and now, by random acts of marketing, sales, and fire extinguishing, that they can never focus on business development.

There is in Grant's approach, as I advocate, both **macro- and micro**-management. In our discussions, he **knew his numbers**, and is **constantly** working at measurable **improvement** in many, many "little things" that, in aggregate, make the difference between ordinary and exceptional profits. The customer experience is **choreographed and scripted**, the sales process (for membership) scripted and supported with good sales aids, and these processes monitored and **enforced**. Overall, he is definitely **in the *marketing* business**, not the tanning business, and devotes the majority of his work time to driving the advertising and marketing. It features **frequency, constancy, the creation/ rotation of different offers,** and the use of multiple media (although **direct mail** is the chief media). He has taken an ordinary business and made it upscale, able to attract and retain affluent clientele but still able to attract a teen to young adult clientele.

For just a moment of self-aggrandizement: Grant told me that he built his entire business—externally, that is, its marketing, and internally, that is, its product/price presentation, sales processes, and so on—based largely on what he gleaned from studying with me, and he has dog-eared, well-worn Kennedy resources going back quite a few years as well as the most recent releases. However, to be fair about it, this is much more about him than me. He has trained himself to be a strong marketer, copywriter, manager, and entrepreneur, and built a multimillion-dollar, premium-price business dominating its local market yet still growing and expanding, and steadily increasing in value. It's a strong testament to what somebody can do if he or she has the will to do it.

Valpak coupon, 2-sided. One side for the tanning salons; the flip side for the fitness club. Both sides shown.

Bounceback postcard—both sides shown. This provides a $10.00 2nd-visit discount. Goes to those who were not sold into membership on first visit. Has tight deadline written in by hand.

In-store(s) flyer for Alternative Membership being tested: $49.95 Keys to the Salon, for any bed (not really—only Bronze through Diamond, not Platinum or Premiere; those are $10.00 additional per session). Note this is a $49.88 per month + $49.00 enrollment fee, 6-month minimum = $348.28 sale.

In-store(s) flyer for Instant Tooth Whitening.

The Power of Premiumization

One of our most impressive Glazer-Kennedy Insider's Circle™ Members is Diana Coutu, co-owner with her husband of Diana's Gourmet Pizzeria, where prices for large pizzas run to $42.99 and her most expensive pizza is $51.99. And no, she's not in Beverly Hills or Manhattan. She's in Winnipeg, Canada. Within a stone's throw, a name-brand discount pizza chain sells pizzas for as little as "2 for $9.99." How can she prosper?

Again, you'll see much of the Ultimate Marketing Plan baked into her business (yes, a pun!)—but neither this chapter nor the black-and-white reproductions of her colorful marketing materials do this story justice, so I urge visiting *www.DianasGourmetPizzeria.ca* to see a lot more.

It might interest you that in the most recent year (still with the recession hanging on), her business doubled and they doubled the store size, added a delivery vehicle, and have more growth cooked up for the next year. Here are some of the biggest contributing factors:

Product Innovation and Premiumization

Several times a month, new or limited-time specialty pizzas are premiered, like Pizza with Brie Cheese and Pears, and Spring Chicken with Mandarin Oranges and Olive Oil. Her regular menu (reproduced in part on the following pages) features classic favorites and unusual gourmet pizzas, plus there are take 'n bake, pizza kits, and even flavored dough balls to make pizza at home from scratch—including Moosehead beer dough and whole-wheat multigrain. They also have pizzas for diabetics, a $150.00 party pizza, plus salads, appetizers, and beverages. By transcending ordinary pizza and with targeted, upscale-oriented marketing, Diana is able to operate a premium pizza business that supports premium pricing (and exceptional profit margins). With her clientele, she is not actually competing with Domino's, Pizza Hut, and the others we all know by name—and that's the big benefit of premiumization of a business.

Another type of product innovation used by Diana is membership. Many customers are in different membership levels and continuity plans, having their credit cards automatically charged a set fee the very first day of every month in exchange for coupons totaling a predetermined value, perks like special phone access, guaranteed delivery even on superbusy days, and special offers. This stabilizes the business' income, locks in customers and discourages them from succumbing to some other pizza store's discounts or advertising, and increases the frequency of purchase per customer. This is basically the same approach as Grant Miller is using at Sun Your Buns. It is a business model we've perfected and teach in great detail to all Glazer-Kennedy Insider's Circle™ Members.

Celebrity and Customer Bragging Rights

The front of her menu tells some of this story. Diana has won Canada's Best Pizza Chef at the world pizza championship in Italy two times, Canada's Best Pizza Chef awards from *Canadian Pizza Magazine* once, and been a judge at the pizza championship games. Her pizzas have taken 4th-Best Pizza 'America's Plate' in New York and have been listed as one of Canada's 30 Best Things from *Reader's Digest*. She has been featured in countless magazines.

None of this is a happy accident. She works hard and invests time and money in staying hot. She is synonymous with premium-pricing pizza and creates demand for her pizzas because of who she is. (As an aside, I teach that most top-income earners are paid as much or more for who they are—manufactured by their deliberate efforts—than what they do or deliver. Make a note.)

If you think making yourself into a celebrity, at least to your targeted customer audience, is beyond you, how do you explain Diana doing it for herself?

Getting, eating, and serving gourmet pizza from a celebrity chef is, for many, a validation of who they are or aspire to be. For those serving it to friends, there is a bragging-rights story to be told. These are significant factors in this business' success, well understood by Diana and included in her own Ultimate Marketing Plan.

All of this ultimately attracts celebrity clientele, too, which enhances the regular customers' bragging-rights story. Serving Diana's pizzas, they are serving the very same pizzas demanded by and catered to Sheryl Crow and Elton John.

Constancy

Finally, Diana is a relentless marketer to her existing customers. She puts out an excellent monthly newsletter, communicates by e-mail and social media, and makes extensive use of postcards, frequently and seasonally. The Thanksgiving postcard shown in this book, for example, was mailed to 1,054 selected customers and 174 were redeemed (about 16 percent) for a profit over costs of $3,847.74 and return on invested dollars of 482 percent. Yes, she knows her numbers. On average, her customers are touched by some marketing media of hers between 24 and 104 times per year.

There you have it: proof that a local, small business in a rather ordinary and crowded category can create celebrity, get publicity, use every media, create profound differentiation, sell at prices substantially higher than competition or industry norms, and thrive.

"Where to go for Gourmet!"

"We can't make every pizza in Winnipeg, so we only make the best"
Your pizza starts with a great tasting crust, sauce & cheese. At Diana's, you can have it anyway you like!

FIRST TIME? TOO MANY CHOICES FOR YOU?

It's okay, all of our pizzas are standard medium crust, marinara sauce & low-fat mozzarella
unless otherwise specified. So just pick your favorite toppings & size, or check out our
Combination, Premium, Supreme & Award Winning Pizzas

HAND TOSSED CRUSTS

Each crust is made from scratch with 100% olive oil
& sea salt for an authentic Italian flavour.

Original - Our most popular crust, made with
unbleached premium white flour.

Whole Wheat - Made with 100% premium whole
wheat flour. Great tasting pizza can be good for you!

Whole Wheat Multigrain - Made with 100%
premium whole wheat flour & a multigrain mix
of cracked wheat, flax seeds, wheat bran, rye
& wheat germs. Available in Med only.

*Deep Dish** - White, whole wheat or Moosehead®
automatically come with triple cheese
- Oh yeah baby, it's all about the coverage!
Available in Med only.

*Gluten-Free** - Made with only gluten-free flours
& yeast. Limited quantities. Available in Med only.

*Moosehead®** - Awarded "Canada's Best Pizza
Crust 2005". Over 1/2 a bottle of Moosehead® Beer
in each crust. A nice crispy outside crust with that
distinctive Moosehead® beer flavour baked into
every bite. Available in Med, Lrg & XL.

* Extra charge applies.

YOUR CHOICE

Medium - The best balance between toppings
& crust. House Favourite!

Thick - Like thick crust? This is for you!

Thin - Less filling, this crust still rises & lets the
cheese & toppings take center stage.

*Crispy Thin*** - This crust is made without yeast
then twice baked for light and crispy texture.
Available in original or 100% whole wheat.
Available in Med & Lg.

**Extra charge applies.

**Med 12" 1.25 • Lg 14" 2.00

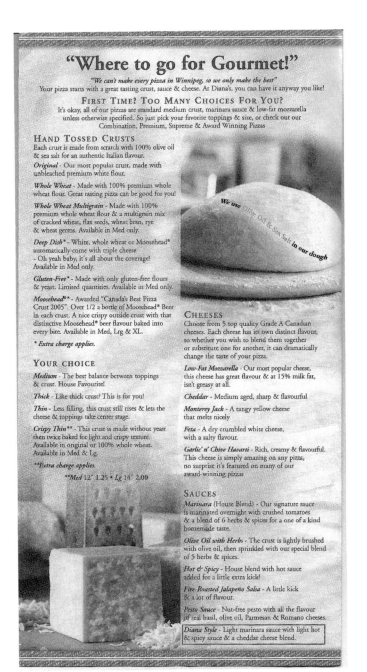

We use Olive Oil & Sea Salt in our dough

CHEESES

Choose from 5 top quality Grade A Canadian
cheeses. Each cheese has its own distinct flavour,
so whether you wish to blend them together
or substitute one for another, it can dramatically
change the taste of your pizza.

Low-Fat Mozzarella - Our most popular cheese,
this cheese has great flavour & at 15% milk fat,
isn't greasy at all.

Cheddar - Medium aged, sharp & flavourful

Monterey Jack - A tangy yellow cheese
that melts nicely

Feta - A dry crumbled white cheese,
with a salty flavour.

Garlic' n' Chive Havarti - Rich, creamy & flavourful.
This cheese is simply amazing on any pizza,
no surprise it's featured on many of our
award-winning pizzas

SAUCES

Marinara (House Blend) - Our signature sauce
is marinated overnight with crushed tomatoes
& a blend of 6 herbs & spices for a one of a kind
homemade taste.

Olive Oil with Herbs - The crust is lightly brushed
with olive oil, then sprinkled with our special blend
of 5 herbs & spices.

Hot & Spicy - House blend with hot sauce
added for a little extra kick!

Fire-Roasted Jalapeño Salsa - A little kick
& a lot of flavour.

Pesto Sauce - Nut-free pesto with all the flavour
of real basil, olive oil, Parmesan & Romano cheeses.

Diana Style - Light marinara sauce with light hot
& spicy sauce & a cheddar cheese blend.

Create Your Own Pizza

5 Sizes to Suit You

	Sm 10"	Med 12"	Lg 14"	XL 16"	Ginormous 18"
CHEESE	10.99	12.99	14.99	17.99	20.99

Did you know? Ginormous 18" Pizza is equal to 1.7 Large Pizzas or 2.5 Mediums!

TOPPINGS

Add any Regular or Gourmet Topping: *Sm* 10" 1.00 • *Med* 12" 2.00 • *Lg* 14" 2.50 • *XL* 16" 3.00 • *Ginormous* 18" 4.00

Regular - Green Peppers, Red Onions, Smoked Ham, Dry Cured Pepperoni, Maple Smoked Crumbled Bacon, 100% Lean Ground Beef, Pineapple, Sliced Fresh Mushrooms, Cold Water Shrimp, Sliced Black Olives, Sliced Green Olives, All - Beef Salami, Italian Sausage & Hot Banana Peppers.

Gourmet - Roma Tomatoes, 100% Lean Seasoned Beef, 100% Lean Hot & Spicy Beef, Spicy Sausage, Jalapeño Peppers, Oven Roasted Red Peppers, Red Peppers, Chopped Spinach, Broccoli, Asparagus, Chick Peas, Sun-Dried Tomatoes, Marinated Artichoke Hearts, Sliced Zucchini, Marinated Spicy Eggplant, Back Bacon, Chorizo Sausage, Green Onions & Julienne Cut Carrots.

Add any Premium Topping: *Sm* 10" 1.50 • *Med* 12" 3.00 • *Lg* 14" 3.75 • *XL* 16" 4.50 • *Ginormous* 18" 6.00

Premium - Fresh Hand Cut Pineapple, BBQ Pulled Pork with a Splash of Hot Sauce, Strip Bacon, Smoked Oysters, Anchovies, All Beef Italian Meatballs, Mild Capicolla Ham, Seasoned Chicken Breast, Pesto Chicken Breast (nut-free), Teriyaki Chicken Breast, Honey Garlic Chicken Breast, BBQ Chicken Breast & Cajun Chicken Breast.

Extra Cheese - 30% more of your favourite cheese • *Double Cheese** - 60% more!
Low Fat Mozzarella, Cheddar, Feta, Monterey Jack, Garlic' n' Chive Havarti, Feta-Jack Blend, Mozza-Jack Blend, Mozza-Cheddar Blend, Mozza-Feta Blend, Cheddar-Feta Blend or 3 Cheese Blend (Mozza, Cheddar, Monterey).

*Counts as 2 toppings.

Combination Pizzas

Any of our Combo Pizzas can be made with Our Award-Winning Moosehead® Beer Crust.
Add 2.00 for Medium, 3.00 for Large & 4.00 for XL.

Sm 10" 13.99 • *Med* 12" 18.99 • *Lg* 14" 22.99 • *XL* 16" 26.99 • *Ginormous* 18" 32.99

CLASSIC VEGETARIAN
Our signature marinara, Fresh mushrooms, green peppers, Roma tomatoes & red onions.

CHEESY
Our signature marinara, low fat mozzarella, medium sharp cheddar & Monterey Jack cheeses.

GOURMET VEGETARIAN
Our signature marinara, chopped spinach, marinated artichoke hearts, sundried tomatoes & red onions.

MEXICAN
Our signature marinara, seasoned beef, Roma tomatoes, medium sharp cheddar & red onions.

HAWAIIAN
Our signature marinara, smoked ham, pineapple & maple smoked crumbled bacon.

BBQ CHICKEN
BBQ sauce, BBQ chicken, maple smoked crumbled bacon & red onions with a cheddar & mozzarella cheese blend.

CANADIAN
Our signature marinara, dry cured pepperoni, sliced fresh mushrooms & maple smoked crumbled bacon.

SPICY MEXICAN
Our signature marinara, hot & spicy beef, Roma tomatoes, jalapeño peppers & medium sharp cheddar.

Award-Winning Pizzas

Med 12" 24.99 • *Lg* 14" 30.99 • *XL* 16" 37.99

BIG D'S BODACIOUS BLT - *"Canada's Best Pizza 2006" - Canadian Pizza Magazine.* No sauce, a blend of medium sharp cheddar & low-fat mozzarella cheeses, capicola ham, strip bacon topped with fresh diced Roma tomatoes, ranch dressing, light pepper & sea salt finished with fresh chopped romaine lettuce on a Moosehead® beer crust.

ULTIMATE PEPPERONI - *"Canada's Best Pizza 2007" - Italian Pizza Games.* Two layers of dry cured pepperoni on a bed of double garlic n' chive havarti & low fat mozzarella cheeses highlighted with our signature sauce on a Moosehead® beer crust.

More Award-Winning Pizzas

	Sm 10"	Med 12"	Lg 14"	XL 16"	Ginormous 18"

THE AWARD WINNER - 23.99 29.99 33.99
"Canada's Best Pizza 2005". Olive oil & herb sauce, smoked ham, red peppers, Roma tomatoes & green olives with a herb medley on a Moosehead® Beer Crust.

HAVARTI HEAVEN 14.99 20.99 24.99 29.99 36.99
"Finalist for Best Pizza 2007". Olive oil & herb sauce, roasted red peppers, red onions, strip bacon & Cajun chicken with a blend of garlic 'n chive havarti & low fat mozzarella cheeses.

RICKY'S REVENGE - 26.99 32.99 39.99 -
A Trailer Park Boys™ Inspired Pizza. Our signature marinara, dry cured pepperoni, chicken fingers, jalapeño peppers, mozzarella & medium sharp cheddar sprinkled with special herbs on a Moosehead® beer crust.

DIANA-SAURUS REX - 34.99 42.99 51.99 -
Our signature marinara, cajun chicken, pepperoni, capicolla ham, strip bacon, all-beef salami, cajun BBQ pulled pork, spicy sausage, extra mozzarella & Monterey Jack on a Moosehead® beer crust.

Specialty Pizzas

Any of our Pizzas can be made with our Award-Winning Moosehead® Beer Crust.
Add 2.00 for Medium, 3.00 for Large & 4.00 for XL.

Sm 10" 15.99 • Med 12" 22.99 • Lg 14" 27.99 • XL 16" 32.99 • Ginormous 18" 40.99

DIANA'S DELUXE - Our signature marinara, green peppers, dry cured pepperoni, fresh mushrooms, maple smoked crumbled bacon & red onions.

BACON DOUBLE CHEESE - Our signature marinara, 100% lean ground beef, maple smoked crumbled bacon, red onions, extra mozzarella & medium sharp cheddar cheese.

SWEET'N'SPICY DIVINE SWINE - Our signature marinara, dry cured pepperoni, fresh hand cut pineapple, BBQ pulled pork with a splash of hot sauce, low fat mozzarella & medium sharp cheddar cheese.

THE CALIFORNIAN - Olive oil & herb sauce, low-fat mozzarella cheese, chopped baby spinach, red onions, seasoned chicken breast, sundried tomatoes & Roma tomatoes.

THE PEPPERONI PIE - Our signature marinara, double topping of dry cured pepperoni & double mozzarella cheese.

ALL MEAT - Our signature marinara, dry cured pepperoni, smoked ham, Italian sausage & maple smoked crumbled bacon.

Premium Pizzas

Sm 10" 16.99 • Med 12" 24.99 • Lg 14" 29.99 • XL 16" 35.99 • Ginormous 18" 44.99

TACO - Fire roasted jalapeño salsa, 100% lean seasoned beef & Roma tomatoes with sliced black olives, drizzled with ranch & baked under our 3 cheese blend of mozzarella, medium sharp cheddar & Monterey Jack cheeses. Served with crisp, chopped Romaine lettuce & taco chips on the side.

SPICY TACO - Fire roasted jalapeño salsa, 100% lean hot & spicy beef, Roma tomatoes & jalapeño peppers with sliced black olives & drizzled with ranch, baked under our 3 cheese blend of mozzarella, medium sharp cheddar & Monterey Jack cheeses. Served with crisp, chopped Romaine lettuce & taco chips on the side.

TONY'S SPICY CHOLULA CHICKEN PIZZA Our signature marinara, Cholula chicken breast, jalapeño peppers, minced garlic, Chorizo sausage & red onions with a dash of paprika.

PIERRE'S PICK - Our signature marinara, mild capicolla ham, oven roasted red peppers, all beef Italian meatballs & strip bacon with mozzarella & medium sharp cheddar cheese.

GREEK - Our signature marinara, green peppers, crumbled feta, black olives, Italian sausage, Roma tomatoes & red onions.

Supreme Pizzas

Sm 10" 17.99 • Med 12" 26.99 • Lg 14" 32.99 • XL 16" 38.99 • Ginormous 18" 48.99

DIANA SUPREME - Our signature marinara, green peppers, dry cured pepperoni, smoked ham, 100% lean cooked ground beef, Italian sausage, fresh mushrooms, pineapple, maple smoked crumbled bacon & onions with double mozzarella.

CHICKEN PARMIGIANA - Extra marinara sauce, sliced breaded chicken breast, extra mozzarella cheese, oregano & basil.

KUNG PAO CHICKEN PIZZA Olive oil & herb sauce, low-fat mozzarella cheese, red peppers, green peppers, red onions, green onions & Kung Pao chicken breast with fresh hand cut pineapple.

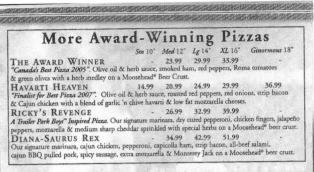

Top Ten Reasons to Give
Diana's Gourmet Pizzeria Gift Certificates
To all Your Friends & Family This Year

10. They always fit.
9. A man has to eat.
8. They fly thru the mail with the greatest of ease.
7. Diana & Pierre have their first baby on the way
6. We'll take care of your friends.
5. Our gift certificates never expire

4. Available in any amount you want.
3. Momma ain't gotta cook- and you still get to eat.
2. Each pizza is handmade, where else can you get custom homemade handmade gifts?
1. It's your great idea.

We think our gift certificates make wonderful presents,
that's why we are sending one to you!

From Diana, Pierre and All of the Staff
At Diana's Gourmet Pizzeria

THANK YOU CERTIFICATE

Diana's Gourmet Pizzeria

Redeemable for: Five dollars off any Large Gourmet Pizza

Not valid with any other offer. Must mention upon ordering.

Diana's
GOURMET PIZZERIA
Not redeemable for cash.

Unit R–730 St. Anne's Road
Winnipeg, MB R2N 0A2
954-7858
www.onegreatpizza.ca
Online Ordering Now Available

Authorized by *DC*

Expires: December 31, 2009

Certificate Code: THKU09

Ultimate Marketing Sins

ULTIMATE MARKETING SIN #1:
Being boring

ULTIMATE MARKETING SIN #2:
Wasting your weaponry aiming at the wrong targets

ULTIMATE MARKETING SIN #3:
Taking your customer's loyalty for granted

ULTIMATE MARKETING SIN #4:
Letting a customer leave angry without first exhausting every means at your disposal to resolve the dispute

Ultimate Marketing
Secret Weapons

ULTIMATE MARKETING SECRET WEAPON #1:
The great USP

ULTIMATE MARKETING SECRET WEAPON #2:
Being clearly understood

ULTIMATE MARKETING SECRET WEAPON #3:
Carefully and thoroughly eliminate all assumptions

ULTIMATE MARKETING SECRET WEAPON #4:
The guts to ask for action every time, in every presentation

ULTIMATE MARKETING SECRET WEAPON #5:
Tailoring and delivering your message to the right target

ULTIMATE MARKETING SECRET WEAPON #6:
Marketing messages developed with the understanding that recipients will be stubbornly reluctant to believe them

ULTIMATE MARKETING SECRET WEAPON #7:
Pictures that prove your case

ULTIMATE MARKETING SECRET WEAPON #8:
Perception congruency

ULTIMATE MARKETING SECRET WEAPON #9:
Constant change

ULTIMATE MARKETING SECRET WEAPON #10:
Capture callers' identity and market to them

ULTIMATE MARKETING SECRET WEAPON #11:
The telephone up-sell

ULTIMATE MARKETING SECRET WEAPON #12:
Telemarketing after direct mail

ULTIMATE MARKETING SECRET WEAPON #13:
Asset sharing for marketing success

ULTIMATE MARKETING SECRET WEAPON #14:
Make the customer feel important, appreciated, and respected

ULTIMATE MARKETING SECRET WEAPON #15:
Developing new products and services for existent customers instead of getting new customers for existent products and services

ULTIMATE MARKETING SECRET WEAPON #16:
Excellence, as desired by the customer

ULTIMATE MARKETING SECRET WEAPON #17:
Enlist a "champion"

Resources from the Author

FREE ULTIMATE MARKETING PLAN "THINK PAGES" ACTION GUIDE can be obtained at *www.NoBSBooks.com*, in the section about this book. You can use this Action Guide to actually create your own Ultimate Marketing Plan for your business.

FREE TRIAL MEMBERSHIP: *LET'S CONTINUE THIS DISCUSSION!* Glazer-Kennedy Insider's Circle™ Members receive my best current ideas, information, strategies, and examples (plus the best current advice from an elite team of offline and online marketing leaders) every month in the NO B.S. MARKETING LETTER plus exclusive online resources, tele-classes, webinars, and audio programs. You can test-drive the complete Membership experience free at: *www.FreeGiftFromUMP.com*

TO DIRECTLY CONTACT THE AUTHOR regarding consulting or copywriting assignments, speaking engagements, or to comment on this book, fax his office at 602-269-3113, or write to him at Kennedy Inner Circle Inc., 15433 N. Tatum Blvd., Suite 104, Phoenix, Arizona 85032. (Do NOT e-mail the author at any of the above websites. The sites are Glazer-Kennedy Insider's Circle™ sites, not his, and he does not get, use, or respond to e-mail.)

Other Books by the Author

The Ultimate Marketing Plan (Adams Media)
The Ultimate Sales Letter (Adams Media)

No B.S. Series from Entrepreneur Press

*No B.S. **Wealth** Attraction in the New Economy*
*No B.S. **Business** Success in the New Economy*
*No B.S. **Sales** Success in the New Economy*
*No B.S. Ruthless **Management** of People and Profits*
*No B.S. **DIRECT Marketing** for NON-Direct Marketing Businesses*
No B.S. Marketing to the Affluent
*No B.S. **Time Management** for Entrepreneurs*

Uncensored Sales Secrets—with Sydney Barrows (Entrepreneur Press)
New Psycho-Cybernetics—with Dr. Maxwell Maltz (Prentice Hall)
Making Them Believe—with Chip Kessler (Glazer-Kennedy Publishing)
Make 'Em Laugh & Take Their Money (Glazer-Kennedy Publishing)

Index